DATA STRUCT

AND

ALGORITHMS

IN **C**

A Comprehensive Guide

MAXWELL RIVERS

ABOUT THIS BOOK

Welcome to "Data Structures and Algorithms in C." This book is designed to be your comprehensive guide to understanding and implementing fundamental data structures and algorithms using the C programming language. Whether you are a beginner looking to build a strong foundation in programming or an experienced developer seeking to deepen your knowledge, this book is crafted to cater to a wide range of readers.

Who is This Book For?

This book is intended for:

- Students: If you are studying computer science or programming, this book will serve as a valuable resource to grasp the core concepts of data structures and algorithms. It will help you excel in your coursework and ace your interviews.
- Programmers: If you are a practicing programmer, this book will sharpen your skills in problem-solving and algorithm design. You will learn how to optimize your code for efficiency and tackle complex tasks with confidence.
- Enthusiasts: If you have a passion for coding and love exploring the intricacies of programming, this book will satisfy your curiosity and provide you with valuable insights into the world of data structures and algorithms.

Why This Book?

Data structures and algorithms are the building blocks of computer programs. They are essential for solving a wide range of computational problems efficiently. This book stands out for several reasons:

1. **C as the Language of Choice:** We have chosen the C programming language for its simplicity and efficiency. C is a powerful language for implementing data structures and algorithms, making it an excellent choice for learners and professionals alike.
2. **Practical Approach:** Throughout the book, you will find practical examples, code snippets, and real-world case studies that bridge the gap between theory and practice. We believe in hands-on learning, and this book is filled with opportunities for you to apply what you've learned.
3. **Comprehensive Coverage:** We cover a wide range of data structures, from arrays and linked lists to trees, graphs, and more. Additionally, we

delve into various sorting and searching algorithms, as well as advanced topics like dynamic programming and NP-completeness.

4. **Performance Analysis:** Understanding the efficiency of algorithms is crucial. We provide clear explanations of time and space complexity analysis using Big O notation, helping you make informed decisions when choosing algorithms for different scenarios.

5. **Case Studies:** Real-world case studies are scattered throughout the book, demonstrating how data structures and algorithms are applied in practical software development. These case studies offer valuable insights into solving real problems.

How to Use This Book

This book is structured to facilitate a progressive learning experience. If you are new to programming or data structures and algorithms, we recommend starting from the beginning and working your way through each chapter sequentially. If you have some prior experience, feel free to skip to the sections that interest you the most or use the book as a reference when tackling specific problems.

We hope you find "Data Structures and Algorithms in C" to be a valuable resource in your journey to becoming a proficient programmer and problem solver. Happy learning!

CONTENTS

INTRODUCTION TO DATA STRUCTURES AND ALGORITHMS

What are Data Structures?

In the world of computer science, data structures are the architectural blueprints that define how data is stored, organized, and accessed within a program. They are the fundamental building blocks upon which the edifice of software applications is constructed. Just as in architecture, where the choice of materials and structure can determine a building's stability and functionality, in computer science, the choice of data structures profoundly influences the efficiency and performance of a program.

Imagine a Library

To illustrate the concept of data structures, let's use a real-world analogy. Think of a library, a place where books are stored and made available for reading. In this analogy:

- **Books** are like data. They contain information, stories, or knowledge that we want to access and use.
- **Bookshelves** are similar to data structures. They provide a way to organize and store books efficiently. Depending on the design of the bookshelves, we can arrange books in various ways, such as by genre, author, or publication date.
- **Library Catalog** serves as a mechanism to access books quickly. It's a tool that helps you find a specific book by its title, author, or subject. This is akin to the algorithms we use to search for and retrieve data from data structures.

Just as a well-organized library enhances the experience of finding and using books, well-designed data structures improve the efficiency of data access and manipulation in a computer program.

The Role of Data Structures

Data structures serve several critical roles in computer programming:

1. **Organization**: They provide a systematic way to store and arrange data. Depending on the data structure chosen, data can be organized hierarchically, linearly, or in other arrangements that suit specific requirements.
2. **Efficiency**: Different data structures offer different trade-offs in terms of time and space efficiency. By selecting the right data structure for a task, you can significantly improve the performance of your program.
3. **Abstraction**: Data structures abstract the underlying complexity of data storage and retrieval. This abstraction simplifies programming, allowing developers to focus on solving problems rather than managing memory.
4. **Reusability**: Many programming languages and libraries come with built-in data structures that you can readily use. Understanding these data structures allows you to leverage existing solutions and write more efficient code.
5. **Problem Solving**: Data structures are essential tools for solving a wide range of computational problems. They enable you to tackle tasks such as searching, sorting, and graph traversal efficiently.

Types of Data Structures

Data structures come in various forms, each suited to specific tasks and scenarios. Some common types of data structures include:

- **Arrays**: Ordered collections of elements, accessed by index.
- **Linked Lists**: Chains of nodes, each containing data and a reference to the next node.
- **Stacks**: Linear data structures with Last-In-First-Out (LIFO) access.
- **Queues**: Linear data structures with First-In-First-Out (FIFO) access.
- **Trees**: Hierarchical structures with nodes and branches, including binary trees, AVL trees, and more.
- **Graphs**: Collections of nodes (vertices) and edges connecting them.
- **Hash Tables**: Key-value data structures for efficient data retrieval.

What are Algorithms?

Algorithms are the secret sauce behind the magic of computer programs. They are the step-by-step instructions that guide a computer in solving a problem or performing a task. Think of them as recipes for computational success, a set of well-defined, precise, and unambiguous instructions that, when followed correctly, lead to the desired outcome.

The Algorithmic World

Algorithms are all around us, often operating behind the scenes in the digital world. When you perform a web search, send an email, or even navigate through your smartphone, algorithms are at work, making decisions, processing data, and optimizing your experience. They are the driving force behind the functionality and efficiency of software applications.

To understand the role of algorithms, consider the following scenarios:

1. **Searching**: When you search for a specific item on an e-commerce website, an algorithm helps find the most relevant results from millions of options in a fraction of a second.
2. **Sorting**: When you organize a list of names in alphabetical order, an algorithm determines the correct arrangement, ensuring efficient access and retrieval.
3. **Navigation**: GPS navigation systems use algorithms to calculate the fastest route from one location to another, taking into account traffic conditions and distance.
4. **Data Analysis**: In scientific research, algorithms are employed to process and analyze massive datasets, helping researchers draw meaningful conclusions.
5. **Encryption**: Algorithms secure your online transactions and communication by encoding and decoding sensitive information.

The Anatomy of an Algorithm

Every algorithm, regardless of its complexity, follows a fundamental structure:

1. **Input**: Algorithms take input data or parameters, which serve as the raw materials for the computation. This input defines the problem to be solved.
2. **Processing**: Algorithms perform a series of well-defined steps to manipulate and process the input data. This is where the real work happens, involving calculations, comparisons, and decisions.

3. **Output**: After processing, an algorithm produces an output or result, which is the solution to the problem. This output could be a value, a report, a sorted list, or any other relevant information.
4. **Termination**: Every algorithm must eventually stop or terminate. It should not run indefinitely. The termination condition ensures that the algorithm does not enter an infinite loop.

The Significance of Algorithms

Algorithms play a pivotal role in computer science and programming for several reasons:

1. **Efficiency**: Algorithms are key to optimizing the use of computational resources, such as time and memory. Well-designed algorithms can dramatically reduce the time it takes to solve a problem or process data.
2. **Problem Solving**: Algorithms provide a structured approach to problem-solving. They break down complex tasks into manageable steps, making it easier to understand and address challenging problems.
3. **Reusability**: Once you've developed an algorithm for a specific task, you can reuse it in various contexts and applications. This promotes code reuse and simplifies software development.
4. **Foundation of Programming**: Algorithms are a fundamental part of programming. Whether you're writing simple scripts or complex software, algorithms are at the core of your code.
5. **Competitive Advantage**: In industries where efficiency and speed matter, having well-optimized algorithms can provide a competitive edge. This is particularly true in fields like finance, data analytics, and gaming.

Importance of Data Structures and Algorithms

Data structures and algorithms are the backbone of computer science and programming. They are the fundamental tools that empower programmers to solve complex problems, create efficient software, and unlock the full potential of computational systems.

1. Efficiency Matters

Efficiency is a core concern in computer programming. Whether you're developing a simple application or a complex system, performance can be a make-or-break factor. Data structures and algorithms play a pivotal role in achieving efficiency in the following ways:

- **Time Complexity**: Different algorithms have different execution times. Understanding the time complexity of an algorithm helps you choose the most efficient one for a specific task.
- **Space Complexity**: Memory usage is a critical consideration, especially in resource-constrained environments. The choice of data structures can impact how efficiently memory is utilized.

By optimizing time and space efficiency, you can ensure that your programs run faster, consume fewer resources, and provide a smoother user experience.

2. Problem Solving and Decision Making

At its core, programming is about solving problems. Data structures and algorithms provide a structured approach to problem-solving:

- **Abstraction**: Data structures abstract the underlying complexities of data storage and retrieval. They simplify the problem-solving process, allowing developers to focus on high-level logic.
- **Divide and Conquer**: Algorithms break down complex problems into smaller, manageable subproblems. This approach makes it easier to tackle intricate challenges step by step.
- **Optimization**: Algorithms aim to find the most efficient way to solve a problem. By using the right algorithm, you can significantly reduce the time and resources required to reach a solution.

3. Versatility and Reusability

The knowledge of data structures and algorithms is transferable. Once you understand these concepts in one programming language, you can apply them to others. This versatility makes you a more adaptable programmer, capable of working with a variety of technologies and platforms.

Moreover, many programming languages and libraries offer built-in data structures and algorithms that you can readily use. Understanding these structures allows you to leverage existing solutions and write more efficient code.

4. Competitive Advantage

In today's technology-driven world, businesses and organizations often rely on software solutions to gain a competitive edge. Efficient algorithms can mean the difference between success and failure, especially in fields such as finance, data analysis, and gaming.

As a programmer or developer, possessing a deep understanding of data structures and algorithms can make you a valuable asset to employers and clients. Your ability to optimize code and solve complex problems efficiently can set you apart from the competition.

5. Academic and Career Growth

For students pursuing computer science or software development, data structures and algorithms are core subjects. Mastery of these concepts is essential not only for academic success but also for excelling in technical interviews and landing job offers.

In the professional world, technical interviews often include questions related to data structures and algorithms. A strong foundation in these areas can open doors to exciting career opportunities in fields like software engineering, data science, artificial intelligence, and more.

Basic Complexity Analysis

Basic complexity analysis is the process of evaluating how an algorithm's performance scales with input size. It helps us answer questions such as:

- How does the running time of an algorithm change as the size of the input data increases?
- How much memory does an algorithm require as the data grows?
- Can we predict how long an algorithm will take to execute based on the size of the input?

These questions are vital because they guide us in selecting the most suitable algorithms and data structures for different tasks. Complexity analysis uses notation like Big O, Omega, and Theta to express an algorithm's time and space complexity.

Time Complexity

Time complexity characterizes the relationship between the size of the input data (n) and the number of basic operations (or steps) an algorithm performs. It provides an upper bound on the algorithm's running time, denoted by Big O notation ($O()$).

Common time complexities include:

- **$O(1)$**: Constant time. The algorithm's execution time remains constant, regardless of the input size.

- **O(log n)**: Logarithmic time. The algorithm's running time grows slowly as the input size increases. Common in efficient search algorithms like binary search.
- **O(n)**: Linear time. The algorithm's running time increases linearly with the input size.
- **O(n log n)**: Linearithmic time. Often seen in efficient sorting algorithms like merge sort and quicksort.
- **O(n^2)**: Quadratic time. The running time grows quadratically with the input size. Common in nested loops.
- **O(2^n)**: Exponential time. Algorithms with this complexity become impractical for large input sizes.

Space Complexity

Space complexity measures the amount of memory an algorithm requires to execute based on the input size. It's also expressed using Big O notation.

Common space complexities include:

- **O(1)**: Constant space. The algorithm uses a fixed amount of memory regardless of input size.
- **O(n)**: Linear space. The memory usage grows linearly with input size.
- **O(n^2)**: Quadratic space. Memory usage increases quadratically with input size.
- **O(log n)**: Logarithmic space. Space usage grows slowly with input size.

It's important to note that time complexity and space complexity aren't always correlated. An algorithm with efficient time complexity may have higher space complexity and vice versa. Therefore, you need to consider both when evaluating algorithms.

Practical Implications

Basic complexity analysis serves as a roadmap for algorithm selection. By understanding the expected time and space complexity of an algorithm, you can make informed decisions about which one to use for a specific task. It also helps you anticipate the algorithm's behavior as data scales, allowing you to optimize your code for real-world scenarios.

BASICS OF C PROGRAMMING

Overview of C Language

C is a powerful and widely-used programming language that has had a profound impact on the world of software development. Developed in the early 1970s by Dennis Ritchie at Bell Labs, C was created as an evolution of the B programming language. It was initially designed to work with the UNIX operating system and has since become the foundation for many other languages and operating systems.

The Popularity of C

C's popularity and longevity can be attributed to several key factors:

1. Efficiency: C provides a high degree of control over computer hardware, making it an efficient choice for system-level programming and applications where performance is critical. It allows developers to write code that executes quickly and uses system resources efficiently.

2. Portability: C code is highly portable, meaning it can be compiled and run on different computer architectures and operating systems with minimal modifications. This portability has made C an ideal choice for developing cross-platform software.

3. Versatility: C is versatile and can be used for a wide range of applications. It's commonly used for systems programming, embedded systems, game development, scientific computing, and more. Its flexibility makes it a valuable tool in the programmer's toolkit.

Key Features of C

To understand the essence of C, it's important to highlight some of its key features:

1. Procedural Language: C is primarily a procedural programming language, which means it relies on procedures (functions) to structure and execute code. This approach promotes modular and maintainable code.

2. Low-Level Access: C provides direct access to computer memory and hardware resources through pointers and low-level constructs. This level of control is essential for system programming.

3. Simple Syntax: C has a simple and minimalistic syntax that emphasizes readability and ease of use. This simplicity allows developers to write concise and efficient code.

4. Standard Library: C comes with a standard library that provides a rich set of functions for performing common tasks, such as input/output operations, string manipulation, and memory allocation.

5. Strongly Typed: C enforces strong typing, meaning that variables must be declared with specific data types before use. This strictness enhances code reliability and safety.

C's Influence on Other Languages

C's design principles and features have influenced the development of many other programming languages. Here are a few notable examples:

- **C++:** An extension of C that introduced object-oriented programming features.
- **C# (C Sharp):** Developed by Microsoft, it incorporates C and C++ features with a focus on simplicity and ease of use.
- **Objective-C:** Known for its use in iOS and macOS development, it combines C with object-oriented features.
- **Java:** While not directly descended from C, Java borrowed C's syntax and added features for platform independence and robustness.

Variables and Data Types

In the world of programming, variables are like containers that hold data. They allow us to store and manipulate information within a program. Understanding variables and data types is fundamental to working with any programming language, including C.

Variables in C

A variable in C is a named storage location in memory that can hold a value. These values can be numbers, characters, or even more complex data structures. Variables have two primary components:

1. Identifier: This is the name of the variable. It's used to access and manipulate the data stored in the variable. Variable names in C must follow specific rules, such as starting with a letter and not being a reserved keyword.

2. Data Type: Every variable in C has a data type that specifies what kind of data it can hold. The data type determines how much memory is allocated for the variable and what operations can be performed on it.

Common Data Types in C

C provides a variety of data types to accommodate different types of data. Here are some common data types in C:

1. Integers (int): Used to store whole numbers. Depending on the platform, int typically uses 2 or 4 bytes of memory.

2. Floating-Point Numbers (float and double): Used to store numbers with decimal points. float typically uses 4 bytes, while double uses 8 bytes for higher precision.

3. Characters (char): Used to store single characters, such as letters, digits, or special symbols. It typically uses 1 byte of memory.

4. Strings (char[] or char*): A sequence of characters. In C, strings are represented as arrays of characters (char[]) or pointers to characters (char*).

5. Boolean (bool): Used to represent true or false values. In C, boolean values are typically implemented using integers, where 0 represents false, and any non-zero value represents true.

6. Void (void): Used as a return type for functions that do not return any value. It's also used for pointer declarations when the pointer type is not specified.

Declaring and Initializing Variables

In C, you declare variables before using them. A declaration tells the compiler the variable's name and data type. Here's how you declare variables:

```
// Syntax: data_type variable_name;
int age;         // Declares an integer variable named 'age'.
float price;     // Declares a floating-point variable named 'price'.
char grade;      // Declares a character variable named 'grade'.
```

You can also initialize variables at the time of declaration:

```
int count = 0;      // Initializes an integer variable 'count' to 0.
float temperature = 98.6;  // Initializes a floating-point variable 'temperature' to 98.6.
char firstLetter = 'A';   // Initializes a character variable 'firstLetter' to 'A'.
```

Variable Naming Conventions

When naming variables in C, it's essential to follow naming conventions for clarity and maintainability. Common conventions include:

- Using descriptive names that indicate the variable's purpose (e.g., totalAmount instead of t).
- Following a consistent naming style, such as camelCase or snake_case (e.g., userName or user_name).
- Avoiding reserved keywords and special characters in variable names.

Control Structures (if-else, loops)

Control structures in programming are used to control the flow of your code. They allow you to make decisions, repeat actions, and create flexible and responsive programs.

Conditional Execution with if-else Statements

The if-else statement in C allows you to make decisions in your code. It provides a way to execute different blocks of code based on a condition. Here's the basic syntax:

```
if (condition) {
    // Code to execute if the condition is true
} else {
    // Code to execute if the condition is false
}
```

For example, you can use if-else to check whether a number is positive or negative:

```
int number = -5;
if (number > 0) {
    printf("The number is positive.\n");
} else {
    printf("The number is negative or zero.\n");
}
```

You can also use multiple if-else statements to create more complex decision-making processes. For instance, you can implement grading logic based on a student's score:

```
int score = 75;
if (score >= 90) {
    printf("Grade: A\n");
} else if (score >= 80) {
    printf("Grade: B\n");
} else if (score >= 70) {
    printf("Grade: C\n");
} else {
    printf("Grade: F\n");
}
```

Looping with for and while Loops

Loops in C allow you to execute a block of code repeatedly as long as a condition is met. There are two common types of loops: for and while.

The for Loop: The for loop is often used when you know how many times you want to repeat a block of code. It consists of three parts: initialization, condition, and update.

```
for (initialization; condition; update) {
    // Code to execute repeatedly
}
```

Here's an example of a for loop that prints numbers from 1 to 5:

```
for (int i = 1; i <= 5; i++) {
    printf("%d ", i);
}
```

The while Loop: The while loop is more flexible and is used when you want to repeat a block of code as long as a condition is true. It checks the condition before executing the code within the loop.

```
while (condition) {
    // Code to execute repeatedly
```

```
}
```

Here's an example of a while loop that prints numbers from 1 to 5:

```
int i = 1;
while (i <= 5) {
    printf("%d ", i);
    i++;
}
```

Functions and Modular Programming

Functions are essential building blocks of modular programming in C. They enable you to break down a complex program into smaller, manageable parts, making your code more organized, reusable, and easier to maintain.

What is a Function?

A function in C is a self-contained block of code that performs a specific task or operation. Functions are designed to be reusable, meaning you can call a function multiple times from different parts of your program. They encapsulate a specific functionality and promote code modularity, which is crucial for writing maintainable and scalable software.

Here's the basic structure of a C function:

```
return_type function_name(parameters) {
    // Function body
    // Code to perform a specific task
    return result; // Optional return statement
}
```

- **return_type**: Specifies the type of value the function returns. If the function doesn't return a value, you use void as the return type.
- **function_name**: The name of the function, which you use to call it from other parts of your program.
- **parameters**: Input values that the function receives and uses to perform its task. Parameters are optional, and a function can have none, one, or multiple parameters.
- **Function body**: Contains the actual code that performs the task. This is enclosed within curly braces {}.
- **return**: An optional statement used to return a value from the function. Not all functions need to return a value.

Function Declaration and Definition

In C, functions are typically declared before they are used. The function declaration informs the compiler about the function's name, return type, and parameter types. The function definition provides the actual implementation of the function.

Here's an example of declaring and defining a simple function that adds two integers:

```
// Function declaration
int add(int a, int b);
```

```
// Function definition
int add(int a, int b) {
    return a + b;
}
```

Calling Functions

To use a function, you call it by its name and provide the required arguments (if any). Here's how you call the add function defined earlier:

```
int result = add(5, 3);
```

Modular Programming Benefits

Modular programming, facilitated by functions, offers several advantages:

1. **Reusability**: Functions can be reused in different parts of your program or even in other projects, saving time and effort.
2. **Readability**: Breaking a program into smaller functions makes it easier to understand, debug, and maintain.
3. **Testing**: You can test individual functions in isolation, making it simpler to identify and fix issues.
4. **Collaboration**: In team environments, modular code allows multiple developers to work on different parts of the program simultaneously.
5. **Scalability**: As your project grows, modular code is easier to extend and adapt to new requirements.

Pointers and Memory Management

Pointers are one of the distinctive features of the C programming language, and they provide a powerful mechanism for working with memory. Understanding pointers and memory management is crucial for writing efficient and flexible C programs.

What is a Pointer?

A **pointer** is a variable that stores the memory address of another variable. Instead of directly containing data, a pointer holds the address where data is located in memory. Pointers allow you to indirectly access and manipulate data in memory, making them a fundamental concept in C programming.

Here's how you declare a pointer variable:

data_type *pointer_name;

- **data_type**: Specifies the type of data that the pointer will point to. For example, an int* pointer points to an integer, and a char* pointer points to a character.
- **pointer_name**: The name of the pointer variable.

To assign a memory address to a pointer, you can use the address-of operator &, which returns the address of a variable:

int x = 42;
int *ptr = &x; // ptr now points to the memory location of 'x'

Dereferencing Pointers

Once you have a pointer that points to a memory location, you can use the dereference operator * to access the value stored at that location:

int value = *ptr; // value now holds the value stored at the memory location pointed to by 'ptr' (42 in this case)

Dynamic Memory Allocation

Pointers are essential for dynamic memory allocation, a feature that allows you to allocate memory during program execution rather than at compile time. C provides two functions for dynamic memory allocation: malloc() and free().

- **malloc()**: This function is used to allocate a block of memory of a specified size. It returns a pointer to the first byte of the allocated memory.

int *arr = (int *)malloc(5 * sizeof(int)); // Allocates memory for an array of 5 integers

- **free()**: Once you're done with dynamically allocated memory, it's important to release it to prevent memory leaks. free() is used to deallocate memory previously allocated by malloc().

free(arr); // Deallocates the dynamically allocated memory

Pointer Arithmetic

Pointers can be manipulated using arithmetic operations. When you perform arithmetic on a pointer, it moves to different memory locations based on the size of the data type it points to. For example:

```
int arr[] = {10, 20, 30, 40, 50};
int *ptr = arr; // 'ptr' points to the first element of 'arr'

// Move to the next element
ptr++; // Now 'ptr' points to the second element (20)

// Access the element using pointer arithmetic
int value = *(ptr + 2); // 'value' holds the value 40 (third element)
```

Pointer Safety and Pitfalls

While pointers offer significant flexibility and control over memory, they can also introduce challenges, such as:

- **Dangling Pointers:** Pointers that point to memory that has been deallocated or no longer exists can lead to undefined behavior.
- **Memory Leaks:** Failing to deallocate dynamically allocated memory with free() can result in memory leaks.
- **Buffer Overflows:** Accessing memory beyond the bounds of an array can lead to unexpected behavior and security vulnerabilities.
- **Null Pointers:** Dereferencing a null pointer (a pointer that doesn't point to valid memory) can result in program crashes.

Proper memory management and careful pointer handling are essential to avoid these issues.

ARRAYS

Introduction to Arrays

Arrays are the workhorses of data storage in programming. They provide a structured and efficient way to store collections of data, whether it's a list of numbers, a set of characters, or even complex objects.

What is an Array?

An **array** is a data structure that allows you to store a collection of elements, all of the same data type, in a contiguous block of memory. Each element in the array is identified by an index or position, starting from 0 for the first element, 1 for the second, and so on. This index is used to access individual elements within the array.

Arrays are versatile and can be used to solve a wide range of problems. They provide a simple and efficient way to work with multiple pieces of data of the same type.

Array Declaration and Initialization

In C, you declare an array by specifying its data type, followed by its name and the number of elements it can hold within square brackets. For example, here's how you declare an array of integers that can hold 5 elements:

int numbers[5];

Once you've declared an array, you can initialize it by specifying its elements' values using curly braces {}:

int numbers[5] = {1, 2, 3, 4, 5};

Alternatively, you can omit the size of the array if you provide an initialization list:

int numbers[] = {1, 2, 3, 4, 5};

In this case, the compiler determines the size of the array based on the number of elements in the initialization list.

Accessing Array Elements

You can access individual elements of an array using square brackets and the element's index. For example, to access the third element of the numbers array declared earlier:

int thirdElement = numbers[2]; // Index 2 corresponds to the third element (3 in this case)

Remember that array indices start from 0, so the first element is at index 0, the second at index 1, and so on.

Arrays and Memory

Arrays are stored in contiguous memory locations. The memory allocated for an array is determined by the size of its data type and the number of elements. This memory layout allows for efficient access and manipulation of array elements.

Array Size and Boundaries

It's essential to manage array sizes carefully to avoid accessing elements beyond the array's boundaries, which can lead to undefined behavior and program crashes. Always ensure that the index used to access an array element falls within the valid range of indices (from 0 to array_size - 1).

Array Operations

Arrays are versatile data structures that enable various operations for organizing, accessing, and manipulating data efficiently.

Accessing Array Elements

Accessing elements within an array is one of the fundamental operations. You use the index of an element to access its value. Remember that array indices in C start from 0 for the first element.

```
int numbers[5] = {10, 20, 30, 40, 50};
int thirdElement = numbers[2]; // Accessing the third element (30)
```

Modifying Array Elements

You can modify the values of array elements by assigning new values using the assignment operator (=).

```
numbers[1] = 25; // Modifying the second element (20 becomes 25)
```

Iterating Over Arrays

Iterating over an array allows you to process all its elements one by one. This is commonly done using loops, such as the for loop or while loop.

```
for (int i = 0; i < 5; i++) {
    printf("%d ", numbers[i]); // Print each element of the 'numbers' array
}
```

Searching in Arrays

Searching for a specific value within an array is a common operation. You can use loops to iterate through the array and compare each element with the value you're searching for.

```
int target = 30;
int found = 0; // A flag to indicate if the target is found

for (int i = 0; i < 5; i++) {
    if (numbers[i] == target) {
        found = 1;
        break; // Exit the loop when the target is found
    }
}

if (found) {
    printf("The target was found in the array.\n");
} else {
    printf("The target was not found in the array.\n");
}
```

Sorting Arrays

Sorting an array arranges its elements in a specific order, such as ascending or descending. Common sorting algorithms like bubble sort, insertion sort, and quicksort are used for this purpose.

```
// Sorting 'numbers' in ascending order using bubble sort
```

```
for (int i = 0; i < 4; i++) {
    for (int j = 0; j < 4 - i; j++) {
        if (numbers[j] > numbers[j + 1]) {
            // Swap elements if they are out of order
            int temp = numbers[j];
            numbers[j] = numbers[j + 1];
            numbers[j + 1] = temp;
        }
    }
}
```

Deleting Elements

Deleting elements from an array typically involves shifting the elements after the deleted element to fill the gap. This can be a complex operation, especially when deleting elements from the middle of an array.

Inserting Elements

Inserting elements into an array also requires shifting elements if there's no space for the new element. Like deletion, this operation can be complex when inserting elements in the middle of an array.

Multi-dimensional Arrays

While one-dimensional arrays are suitable for storing linear collections of data, many real-world problems involve more complex data structures with multiple dimensions. Multi-dimensional arrays provide a powerful solution for such scenarios, allowing you to represent data in a grid-like fashion.

What are Multi-dimensional Arrays?

A **multi-dimensional array** in C is an array of arrays or, more generally, a collection of elements organized in multiple dimensions. You can think of it as a matrix or a table with rows and columns. Multi-dimensional arrays are used to represent data that naturally fits into a two-dimensional grid or higher-dimensional structures.

Common use cases for multi-dimensional arrays include:

- **Matrices:** Representing mathematical matrices used in linear algebra and computer graphics.
- **Tables:** Storing tabular data, such as spreadsheets or databases.
- **Images:** Representing pixel data in images, where each element of the array corresponds to a pixel's color value.

- **3D Graphics:** Storing 3D models, where each element represents a point in space.

Two-dimensional Arrays

The most common form of multi-dimensional arrays in C is the two-dimensional array. It's essentially an array of arrays, where each row is an array of elements, and the entire structure forms a grid.

To declare a two-dimensional array, you specify the data type, the array name, and the dimensions:

```
data_type array_name[row_size][column_size];
```

Here's an example of a 3x3 integer matrix:

```
int matrix[3][3];
```

You can also initialize a two-dimensional array when you declare it:

```
int matrix[3][3] = {
    {1, 2, 3},
    {4, 5, 6},
    {7, 8, 9}
};
```

Accessing elements in a two-dimensional array requires specifying both the row and column indices:

```
int element = matrix[1][2]; // Accesses the element in the second row and third column (6 in this case)
```

Multi-dimensional Arrays Beyond 2D

While two-dimensional arrays are the most common, C supports multi-dimensional arrays with more than two dimensions. For instance, a three-dimensional array can be used to represent a cube of data, where each element is identified by three indices.

```
int cube[2][3][4]; // A 3D array with dimensions 2x3x4
```

Accessing elements in multi-dimensional arrays with more than two dimensions involves specifying the indices for each dimension.

Array Sorting and Searching Algorithms

Arrays are at the heart of many data processing tasks, and sorting and searching are among the most common operations performed on arrays.

Array Sorting Algorithms

Sorting is the process of arranging elements in a specific order, such as ascending or descending. Properly sorted data is essential for efficient searching, reporting, and data analysis. Several sorting algorithms exist, each with its advantages and trade-offs. Here are some commonly used sorting algorithms:

1. **Bubble Sort:** This simple algorithm repeatedly steps through the list, compares adjacent elements, and swaps them if they are in the wrong order. The pass-throughs continue until no swaps are needed, indicating that the list is sorted.
2. **Selection Sort:** Selection sort divides the input list into two parts: the sorted part and the unsorted part. It repeatedly selects the minimum (or maximum) element from the unsorted part and moves it to the sorted part.
3. **Insertion Sort:** In insertion sort, the array is divided into a sorted and an unsorted region. The algorithm repeatedly takes an element from the unsorted region and inserts it into its correct position within the sorted region.
4. **Merge Sort:** Merge sort is a divide-and-conquer algorithm that divides the unsorted list into n sublists, each containing one element. It then repeatedly merges sublists to produce new sorted sublists until there is only one sublist remaining, which is the sorted list.
5. **Quick Sort:** Quick sort is another divide-and-conquer algorithm. It selects a 'pivot' element and partitions the other elements into two sub-arrays according to whether they are less than or greater than the pivot. The sub-arrays are then sorted recursively.
6. **Heap Sort:** Heap sort uses a binary heap data structure to build a max-heap or min-heap, depending on whether you want ascending or descending order. It then repeatedly extracts the root element (which is the largest or smallest) and rebuilds the heap until the array is sorted.

Array Searching Algorithms

Searching is the process of finding a specific element within an array. Various searching algorithms exist, each with its efficiency characteristics. Here are some common searching algorithms:

1. **Linear Search:** Linear search, also known as sequential search, checks each element in the array one by one until the target element is found. It is simple but may be inefficient for large datasets.
2. **Binary Search:** Binary search is an efficient algorithm for finding a target element in a sorted array. It repeatedly divides the search interval in half until the target is found or the search interval is empty.
3. **Hashing:** Hashing involves using a hash function to map keys to locations in an array (hash table). It allows for fast retrieval of data when the key is known.
4. **Interpolation Search:** Interpolation search is an improved version of binary search that works well when the data is uniformly distributed. It estimates the position of the target element based on the values of the endpoints and interpolates its probable location.
5. **Jump Search:** Jump search is similar to linear search but divides the array into smaller blocks and uses a step size to skip ahead in the search process. It combines the efficiency of binary search with the simplicity of linear search.

Choosing the Right Algorithm

The choice of sorting and searching algorithms depends on various factors, including the size of the dataset, whether the data is already partially sorted, and the desired efficiency. Understanding the strengths and weaknesses of different algorithms is essential for selecting the most suitable one for a specific task.

LINKED LISTS

Introduction to Linked Lists

Linked lists are a fundamental and versatile data structure used in computer science and programming. Unlike arrays, which store elements in contiguous memory locations, linked lists organize elements as a chain of nodes, each containing data and a reference (or link) to the next node in the sequence. This unique structure makes linked lists flexible and efficient for various tasks.

What is a Linked List?

At its core, a **linked list** is a collection of elements, called nodes, where each node consists of two parts: data and a reference (or pointer) to the next node in the sequence. This reference links the nodes together, forming a linear or sequential data structure.

Here's a basic visual representation of a singly linked list:

```lua
 +---+   +---+   +---+
 | 1 | -> | 2 | -> | 3 |
 +---+   +---+   +---+
```

In this example, each node contains a value (1, 2, or 3) and a reference to the next node. The last node typically points to a special value, often called "null" or "None," indicating the end of the list.

Linked List Advantages

Linked lists offer several advantages over other data structures like arrays:

1. **Dynamic Size:** Linked lists can dynamically grow or shrink, making them suitable for situations where the size of the data structure is unknown in advance.
2. **Efficient Insertions and Deletions:** Inserting or deleting elements in a linked list is often more efficient than in arrays because it requires updating only a few pointers.
3. **Memory Efficiency:** Linked lists allocate memory for each element individually, reducing memory wastage.
4. **No Contiguous Memory Requirement:** Unlike arrays, linked lists do not require contiguous memory locations, making them suitable for systems with fragmented memory.

Types of Linked Lists

There are different types of linked lists, each with its unique characteristics:

1. **Singly Linked Lists:** In a singly linked list, each node points to the next node in the sequence, forming a unidirectional chain.
2. **Doubly Linked Lists:** Doubly linked lists extend singly linked lists by adding a backward reference to each node, allowing for bidirectional traversal.
3. **Circular Linked Lists:** Circular linked lists are like singly or doubly linked lists, but the last node points back to the first, forming a closed loop.

When to Use Linked Lists

Linked lists are particularly useful in situations where:

- The size of the data structure is unknown or can change over time.
- Frequent insertions and deletions of elements are required.
- Contiguous memory is not readily available or is inefficient to use.

Understanding linked lists and their variants is essential as they serve as the foundation for more complex data structures like stacks, queues, and hash tables.

Singly Linked Lists

Singly linked lists are a fundamental type of linked list data structure. In a singly linked list, each node contains two parts: the data and a reference (or link) to the next node in the sequence. This reference points to the next node in the list, forming a unidirectional chain. Singly linked lists are widely used in computer science and programming due to their simplicity and efficiency for certain operations.

Structure of a Singly Linked List

A singly linked list consists of nodes, where each node contains two parts:

1. **Data:** This part holds the value or data that the node represents.
2. **Next Reference:** This reference (or pointer) points to the next node in the list. It's essential for maintaining the sequence of nodes.

Here's a visual representation of a singly linked list:

```
+---+   +---+   +---+   +---+
| 1 | -> | 2 | -> | 3 | -> | 4 |
+---+   +---+   +---+   +---+
```

In this example, each node contains a value (1, 2, 3, or 4) and a reference to the next node in the sequence.

Key Operations on Singly Linked Lists

Singly linked lists support various operations for manipulating data. Here are some of the essential operations:

1. **Insertion:** You can add a new node to the list at the beginning (prepend), end (append), or at a specific position (insert).
2. **Deletion:** You can remove a node from the list by updating the references. Deletion can be done at the beginning, end, or at a specific position.
3. **Traversal:** To access and process all elements in the list, you can use traversal. This typically involves starting from the head (the first node) and moving through the list node by node.
4. **Search:** You can search for a specific value within the list by traversing it and comparing values until a match is found or the end of the list is reached.

Advantages and Disadvantages

Singly linked lists offer several advantages:

- Dynamic Size: Singly linked lists can grow or shrink in size as needed.
- Efficient Insertions and Deletions: Adding or removing elements at the beginning is efficient because it requires updating only a few references.
- Memory Efficiency: Memory is allocated for each element individually, reducing waste.

However, they also have some limitations:

- Bidirectional Traversal: Singly linked lists only support forward traversal. For backward traversal, you'd typically use a doubly linked list.
- Random Access: Unlike arrays, singly linked lists do not support direct random access to elements. Accessing an element requires traversing the list from the beginning.

Applications

Singly linked lists find applications in various scenarios, including:

- Implementing stacks and queues.
- Managing data structures for symbol tables and hash tables.
- Representing sparse matrices efficiently.
- Handling memory allocation and deallocation in dynamic memory management.

Doubly Linked Lists

Doubly linked lists are a variation of linked lists that extend the capabilities of singly linked lists. In a doubly linked list, each node contains three parts: the data, a reference (or link) to the next node, and a reference to the previous node. This bidirectional linking allows for efficient traversal in both directions. Doubly linked lists find applications in various scenarios where forward and backward traversal are essential.

Structure of a Doubly Linked List

In a doubly linked list, each node has three parts:

1. **Data:** This part holds the value or data that the node represents.
2. **Next Reference:** This reference points to the next node in the sequence, just like in a singly linked list.
3. **Previous Reference:** This reference points to the previous node in the sequence, allowing bidirectional traversal.

Here's a visual representation of a doubly linked list:

```
  +---+   +---+   +---+   +---+
<- | 1 | < | 2 | < | 3 | < | 4 | ->
  +---+   +---+   +---+   +---+
```

In this example, each node contains a value (1, 2, 3, or 4), a reference to the next node (pointing to the right), and a reference to the previous node (pointing to the left).

Key Operations on Doubly Linked Lists

Doubly linked lists support a range of operations similar to singly linked lists. These operations include:

1. **Insertion:** You can add a new node to the list at the beginning (prepend), end (append), or at a specific position (insert).
2. **Deletion:** Removing a node from the list is efficient due to bidirectional links. Deletion can occur at the beginning, end, or at a specific position.
3. **Traversal:** Bidirectional traversal is a significant advantage, allowing you to move both forward and backward through the list.
4. **Search:** You can search for a specific value within the list by traversing it in either direction.

Advantages and Disadvantages

Doubly linked lists offer several advantages over singly linked lists:

- Bidirectional Traversal: The ability to traverse both forward and backward is valuable in many scenarios.
- Efficient Deletions: Deletion of a node is more efficient in a doubly linked list since it can be done without traversing from the beginning.

However, they also have some trade-offs:

- Increased Memory Usage: The additional previous reference consumes more memory than singly linked lists.
- More Complex Implementation: Managing bidirectional references adds complexity to the implementation.

Applications

Doubly linked lists find applications in situations where bidirectional traversal is required, including:

- Implementing advanced data structures like deque (double-ended queue) and the linked list component of a hash table.
- Implementing text editors with undo and redo functionality, as it allows efficient backward and forward navigation through the editing history.

- Implementing various algorithms where efficient traversal in both directions is advantageous.

Circular Linked Lists

Circular linked lists are a variation of linked lists where the last node points back to the first, forming a closed loop. This unique characteristic makes circular linked lists suitable for scenarios where continuous access to elements in a loop is required.

Structure of a Circular Linked List

In a circular linked list, each node contains two parts:

1. **Data:** This part holds the value or data that the node represents.
2. **Next Reference:** This reference points to the next node in the sequence. Unlike traditional linked lists, the last node's next reference points back to the first node, closing the loop.

Here's a visual representation of a circular linked list:

```
   +---+   +---+   +---+
-->| 1 |-->| 2 |-->| 3 |
|  +---+   +---+   +---+
|   ^                |
+----|--------------+
```

In this example, each node contains a value (1, 2, or 3), and the last node's next reference points back to the first node, creating a circular structure.

Key Operations on Circular Linked Lists

Circular linked lists support operations similar to other linked lists, with the added advantage of looping around seamlessly. These operations include:

1. **Insertion:** You can insert a new node at the beginning (prepend), end (append), or at a specific position (insert), just like in other linked lists.
2. **Deletion:** Removing a node from the list can be done efficiently due to the circular structure. Deletion can occur at the beginning, end, or at a specific position.
3. **Traversal:** Traversing a circular linked list allows you to move continuously through the list, looping back to the beginning when you reach the end.
4. **Search:** You can search for a specific value within the list by traversing it in a loop, taking advantage of the circular structure.

Advantages and Disadvantages

Circular linked lists offer some advantages and unique characteristics:

- Continuous Looping: The circular structure allows for continuous looping through the list, making them suitable for applications where elements need to be processed cyclically.
- Efficient Operations: Due to the circular nature, insertions and deletions are often efficient, especially when dealing with the first or last node.

However, they also have some considerations:

- Extra Complexity: Managing the circular aspect of the list can add complexity to implementation.
- Determining Termination: Care must be taken when traversing a circular linked list to ensure that loops terminate correctly.

Applications

Circular linked lists find applications in various scenarios where continuous looping is required, including:

- Circular buffers: Used in embedded systems and real-time processing to continuously cycle through data.
- Round-robin scheduling algorithms: In operating systems, circular linked lists can be used to manage and allocate resources in a rotating fashion.
- Games and simulations: Circular linked lists can simulate actions that repeat in a loop, such as game character movement or animation frames.

Operations on Linked Lists

Linked lists are versatile data structures that support a variety of operations for managing and manipulating their elements. Understanding these operations is essential for effectively working with linked lists in your programs.

1. Insertion

- **Insert at the Beginning (Prepend):** This operation involves adding a new node to the beginning of the linked list. It's a quick and efficient operation, as it only requires updating the head pointer.

- **Insert at the End (Append):** Appending a node adds it to the end of the linked list. While it's a straightforward operation, it may involve traversing the entire list to find the last node, making it less efficient for long lists.
- **Insert at a Specific Position:** You can insert a node at a specific position within the list by updating the pointers of the neighboring nodes. This operation is useful when you need to maintain a sorted order in the list.

2. Deletion

- **Delete at the Beginning:** Deleting the first node in the list involves updating the head pointer to point to the second node and freeing the memory of the old head.
- **Delete at the End:** Removing the last node may require traversing the entire list to find the second-to-last node, updating its next pointer to NULL, and freeing the memory of the last node.
- **Delete a Specific Node:** Deleting a node at a particular position involves updating the next pointer of the previous node to skip the target node and then freeing the memory of the target node.

3. Traversal

- **Forward Traversal:** You can traverse a linked list from the beginning (head) to the end, visiting each node one by one. This is the most common form of traversal and is used for operations like printing the list or searching for a specific element.
- **Backward Traversal (for Doubly Linked Lists):** In doubly linked lists, you can traverse the list both forward and backward, as each node has references to both the next and previous nodes.

4. Search

- **Linear Search:** To search for a specific value within the list, you can perform a linear search by traversing the list and comparing each node's value with the target value.
- **Binary Search (for Sorted Lists):** If the linked list is sorted, you can apply binary search techniques to locate the target element more efficiently. However, this requires maintaining a sorted order in the list.

5. Length (Counting Nodes)

- To determine the number of nodes in a linked list, you can traverse the list while keeping a count of nodes encountered. This count represents the length of the linked list.

6. Concatenation

- You can concatenate two linked lists by linking the last node of the first list to the head of the second list. This operation combines the elements of both lists into a single list.

7. Reversal

- Reversing a linked list involves changing the direction of the links, so the last node becomes the new head, and the old head becomes the last node. This operation is often used in various algorithms and data manipulations.

8. Merging (for Sorted Lists)

- When dealing with two sorted linked lists, you can merge them into a single sorted list. This is a common operation in algorithms like merge sort and for combining results in database operations.

9. Cyclic Detection

- Detecting cycles or loops in a linked list is crucial to prevent infinite loops. Algorithms like Floyd's cycle-finding algorithm can determine whether a linked list contains a cycle.

Understanding these operations provides you with the tools needed to work with linked lists effectively. Depending on your specific use case and requirements, you may choose and combine these operations to perform more complex tasks and solve various programming challenges. Linked lists serve as the foundation for many other data structures and algorithms, making them a valuable concept to master.

Linked List Sorting and Searching

Linked lists, with their dynamic structure, can be sorted and searched efficiently using various algorithms. Sorting and searching are fundamental operations in data manipulation and retrieval, and understanding how to perform them on linked lists is essential for effective programming.

Sorting Linked Lists

Sorting a linked list involves rearranging its elements in a specific order, such as ascending or descending. Here are a few common sorting algorithms used for linked lists:

1. **Merge Sort:** Merge sort is a popular algorithm for sorting linked lists. It's based on the divide-and-conquer principle and involves dividing the list into halves, sorting each half, and then merging the sorted halves back together.
2. **Insertion Sort:** Although not as efficient as merge sort for large lists, insertion sort can be applied to linked lists. It iterates through the list and inserts each element into its correct position in the sorted portion of the list.
3. **Selection Sort:** Similar to insertion sort, selection sort can be adapted for linked lists. It repeatedly selects the smallest element from the unsorted portion of the list and appends it to the sorted portion.
4. **Bubble Sort:** While less efficient than other sorting algorithms, bubble sort can be implemented for linked lists by repeatedly swapping adjacent elements that are out of order.

Searching Linked Lists

Searching in linked lists involves locating a specific element within the list. Common searching algorithms for linked lists include:

1. **Linear Search:** Linear search is a straightforward method where you traverse the linked list from the beginning, comparing each element with the target value until you find a match or reach the end of the list.
2. **Binary Search (for Sorted Lists):** If the linked list is sorted, binary search can be applied efficiently. However, this requires maintaining the sorted order of the list.
3. **Hashing:** Hashing is a technique that can be used when searching for specific elements. It involves hashing the value to be searched and using the resulting hash code to access the corresponding node. This is often used in hash tables.
4. **Floyd's Cycle-Finding Algorithm (for Cycle Detection):** Floyd's algorithm is employed to detect cycles in a linked list. It can determine whether a linked list contains a loop or is acyclic.

Complexity Analysis

The efficiency of sorting and searching algorithms for linked lists can vary significantly. It's crucial to consider the time and space complexity of each algorithm to choose the most suitable one for your specific use case.

- **Merge Sort:** Merge sort offers an efficient time complexity of $O(n \log n)$ for linked lists. It is a stable sorting algorithm and works well for large lists.
- **Insertion Sort and Selection Sort:** These algorithms have a time complexity of $O(n^2)$ in the worst case, which makes them less suitable for large lists.

- **Binary Search:** For sorted linked lists, binary search offers a time complexity of $O(\log n)$. However, the list must be sorted initially, which may add extra time.
- **Linear Search:** Linear search has a time complexity of $O(n)$, making it suitable for unsorted linked lists or when the search criteria are not based on value but on other factors.

Understanding the strengths and weaknesses of each algorithm and choosing the right one for your specific scenario is crucial for optimizing performance and efficiency when working with linked lists.

STACKS AND QUEUES

Introduction to Stacks

In the world of computer science and programming, stacks are a fundamental data structure that follows a unique and intuitive principle: **Last-In, First-Out (LIFO)**. Much like a stack of books or plates, where the last item placed on top is the first one to be removed, a stack data structure operates in a similar manner. It's a versatile tool with a wide range of applications across various domains.

What is a Stack?

At its core, a **stack** is a linear data structure that consists of a collection of elements. However, it distinguishes itself by the way elements are added and removed. In a stack, elements are added or removed from only one end, which is often referred to as the "top."

Imagine a physical stack of plates. When you add a new plate, it goes on top of the existing stack. When you need to remove a plate, you take the one from the top. This characteristic makes the stack operate in a **Last-In, First-Out (LIFO)** fashion, where the most recently added item is the first one to be removed.

Key Characteristics of Stacks

Stacks exhibit the following key characteristics:

1. **LIFO Principle:** The most recently added item is the first to be removed, making the stack behave like a spring-loaded stack of items.

2. **Limited Access:** In a stack, you can only add or remove items from the top. You cannot directly access or manipulate elements in the middle of the stack without first removing the elements above.

3. **Dynamic Size:** Stacks can dynamically grow or shrink to accommodate elements as needed, making them suitable for situations where the size of the data structure is unknown in advance.

Common Operations on Stacks

Stacks support a set of fundamental operations:

1. **Push:** Adding an item to the top of the stack is called "push." This operation places a new element onto the stack.

2. **Pop:** Removing the item from the top of the stack is referred to as "pop." This operation removes and returns the top element.

3. **Peek (or Top):** Peek allows you to view the top element without removing it from the stack. It's a read-only operation.

4. **isEmpty:** You can check whether the stack is empty or not using this operation. An empty stack has no elements.

Applications of Stacks

Stacks have a wide range of applications in computer science and programming, including:

- **Function Calls:** Stacks are used to manage function calls and their associated variables and return addresses.
- **Expression Evaluation:** Stacks play a critical role in evaluating expressions, such as arithmetic expressions and postfix notation (Reverse Polish Notation).
- **Undo Mechanisms:** Stacks can be used to implement undo and redo functionality in applications.
- **Backtracking Algorithms:** Algorithms that require backtracking, like depth-first search (DFS), often use stacks to manage state.
- **Memory Management:** Stacks are used for managing memory in runtime environments like the call stack in a programming language.

Implementing Stacks in C

Stacks are a fundamental data structure that can be implemented efficiently in the C programming language. To create a stack in C, you can use an array or a linked list as the underlying data structure.

Array-Based Stack Implementation

An array-based stack is a simple and efficient way to implement a stack in C. Here's a step-by-step guide to creating an array-based stack:

1. **Define the Stack Size:** Determine the maximum number of elements the stack can hold and declare an array of that size. For example, to create a stack that can hold integers, you can use:

```c
#define MAX_SIZE 100
int stack[MAX_SIZE];
int top = -1; // Initialize the top pointer
```

• **Push Operation:** To push an element onto the stack, increment the top pointer and assign the value to the corresponding index in the array.

```c
void push(int value) {
   if (top < MAX_SIZE - 1) {
      stack[++top] = value;
   } else {
      printf("Stack overflow: Cannot push element %d\n", value);
   }
}
```

• **Pop Operation:** To pop an element from the stack, return the element at the current top index and then decrement the top pointer.

```c
int pop() {
   if (top >= 0) {
      return stack[top--];
   } else {
      printf("Stack underflow: Stack is empty\n");
      return -1; // You can choose to return a specific value to indicate an empty stack.
   }
}
```

• **Peek Operation:** To peek at the top element without removing it, simply return the element at the current top index.

```c
int peek() {
   if (top >= 0) {
      return stack[top];
   } else {
      printf("Stack is empty\n");
      return -1; // You can choose to return a specific value to indicate an empty stack.
   }
}
```

- **isEmpty Operation:** You can check if the stack is empty by examining the value of top.

```
int isEmpty() {
    return top == -1;
}
```

Linked-List-Based Stack Implementation

Another way to implement a stack in C is by using a linked list. This approach offers dynamic memory allocation and can handle a variable number of elements. Here's how to implement a linked-list-based stack:

- **Define a Node Structure:** Start by defining a structure for the nodes in the linked list. Each node should contain the data and a pointer to the next node.

```
struct Node {
    int data;
    struct Node* next;
};
```

- **Initialize the Stack:** Declare a pointer to the top of the stack and initialize it to NULL to indicate an empty stack.

```
struct Node* top = NULL;
```

- **Push Operation:** To push an element onto the stack, allocate memory for a new node, assign the value, and update the next pointer to point to the current top node. Then, update the top pointer to the new node.

```
void push(int value) {
    struct Node* newNode = (struct Node*)malloc(sizeof(struct Node));
    if (newNode == NULL) {
        printf("Memory allocation failed\n");
        return;
    }
    newNode->data = value;
    newNode->next = top;
    top = newNode;
}
```

- **Pop Operation:** To pop an element from the stack, first check if the stack is empty. If not, remove the top node, free its memory, and update the top pointer to the next node.

```
int pop() {
    if (isEmpty()) {
        printf("Stack is empty\n");
        return -1; // You can choose to return a specific value to indicate an empty stack.
```

```
    }
    struct Node* temp = top;
    int value = temp->data;
    top = top->next;
    free(temp);
    return value;
}
```

- **Peek Operation:** To peek at the top element without removing it, simply return the data in the top node.

```
int peek() {
    if (isEmpty()) {
        printf("Stack is empty\n");
        return -1; // You can choose to return a specific value to indicate an empty stack.
    }
    return top->data;
}
```

- **isEmpty Operation:** You can check if the stack is empty by examining the top pointer.

```
int isEmpty() {
    return top == NULL;
}
```

Choosing Between Array-Based and Linked-List-Based Stacks

The choice between an array-based and a linked-list-based stack depends on your specific requirements. Here are some factors to consider:

- **Memory Usage:** Array-based stacks allocate memory upfront, while linked-list-based stacks allocate memory dynamically as needed. If memory usage is a concern, a linked list might be more efficient.
- **Maximum Capacity:** Array-based stacks have a maximum capacity defined by the array size, while linked-list-based stacks can grow dynamically. If you need a stack with a flexible size, a linked list is a better choice.
- **Insertion/Deletion Efficiency:** Array-based stacks are typically more efficient for small to medium-sized stacks due to constant-time insertions and deletions. Linked-list-based stacks have a constant-time push operation but may involve memory allocation and deallocation, which can introduce overhead.
- **Ease of Implementation:** Array-based stacks are relatively straightforward to implement, while linked-list-based stacks involve more complex memory management.
- **Error Handling:** Array-based stacks can run into overflow errors if the stack size exceeds the predefined capacity. Linked-list-based stacks can run into memory allocation errors if the system is out of memory.

Consider your specific use case and performance requirements when choosing between these implementations. Both can be valuable tools in different scenarios, and mastering both will enhance your ability to tackle a variety of programming challenges effectively.

Stack Applications

Stacks, with their Last-In, First-Out (LIFO) behavior, find applications across various domains in computer science and programming. Their simplicity and efficiency make them valuable tools for solving a wide range of problems.

1. Function Call Management

One of the primary applications of stacks is managing function calls in programs. When a function is called, its local variables, return address, and other relevant information are pushed onto the stack. When the function completes its execution, this information is popped from the stack, allowing the program to return to the caller. This mechanism enables the implementation of recursion and keeps track of function call hierarchies.

2. Expression Evaluation

Stacks are essential for evaluating expressions, including arithmetic expressions and postfix notation (Reverse Polish Notation, or RPN). In the case of arithmetic expressions, stacks can be used to convert infix expressions to postfix notation, making evaluation more efficient. RPN expressions can be directly evaluated using a stack.

3. Undo and Redo Functionality

Many applications, such as text editors and graphic design software, employ stacks to implement undo and redo functionality. Each action performed by the user, such as typing, formatting, or drawing, is pushed onto a stack. When the user invokes the undo operation, the most recent action is popped from the stack, effectively reversing the operation. Redoing an action pushes it back onto the stack.

4. Backtracking Algorithms

Backtracking algorithms, used in various problem-solving scenarios like solving puzzles and searching through decision trees, often rely on stacks to manage states and explore different paths. As the algorithm explores a path, it pushes the current state onto the stack and pops it to backtrack when necessary.

5. Memory Management

In low-level programming languages like C and C++, stacks are instrumental for managing memory allocation and deallocation. The call stack keeps track of local variables and function call information, allowing for efficient memory management.

6. Expression Parsing

Parsing and interpreting complex expressions or languages often involve using stacks to track the nesting of brackets, parentheses, and other delimiters. Stacks help ensure that expressions are properly balanced and can also assist in evaluating expressions.

7. Algorithm Implementations

Stacks are integral to various algorithms, including depth-first search (DFS) for graph traversal, as they help maintain a list of nodes to explore. Stacks are also used in the implementation of other data structures and algorithms, such as the evaluation of postfix expressions.

8. Data Structure Implementations

Stacks are sometimes used as building blocks for implementing other data structures. For instance, they can be used to simulate the behavior of a stack-based machine, which is fundamental in creating virtual machines and interpreters for programming languages.

9. Undo and Redo Operations in Software

In software development, developers often use version control systems like Git. Stacks are employed to manage changes to source code. Commits and changesets are added to the stack, and operations like "git commit" and "git reset" use stack principles to manage changes to the codebase.

Introduction to Queues

In computer science and programming, queues are a fundamental data structure that follows a unique and intuitive principle: **First-In, First-Out (FIFO)**. Queues provide an ordered and organized way to manage data, making them invaluable for various applications across different domains.

What is a Queue?

A **queue** is a linear data structure that represents an ordered collection of elements. Unlike arrays or lists, where elements can be inserted or removed from both ends, queues have specific rules for inserting and removing elements. In a queue, elements are added at one end, called the "rear" or "tail," and removed from the other end, called the "front" or "head."

Imagine a real-world queue of people waiting in line. The person who joins the queue first is the first to leave. Queues operate in a **First-In, First-Out (FIFO)** manner, mirroring this real-world scenario.

Key Characteristics of Queues

Queues exhibit the following key characteristics:

1. **FIFO Principle:** The first element added to the queue is the first to be removed. This ensures that elements are processed in the order they were added.
2. **Limited Access:** In a queue, you can only add elements at the rear and remove elements from the front. Elements in the middle cannot be directly accessed or removed.
3. **Dynamic Size:** Queues can dynamically grow or shrink to accommodate elements as needed, making them suitable for scenarios where the size of the data structure is unknown in advance.

Common Operations on Queues

Queues support a set of fundamental operations:

1. **Enqueue (or Push):** Adding an element to the rear of the queue is called "enqueue" or "push." This operation is used to insert elements into the queue.
2. **Dequeue (or Pop):** Removing an element from the front of the queue is referred to as "dequeue" or "pop." This operation removes and returns the front element.
3. **Peek (or Front):** Peek allows you to view the front element without removing it from the queue. It's a read-only operation.
4. **isEmpty:** You can check whether the queue is empty or not using this operation. An empty queue has no elements.

Applications of Queues

Queues have a wide range of applications in computer science and programming, including:

- **Task Scheduling:** In operating systems, queues are used to schedule processes for execution. The process at the front of the queue is given priority and executed first.
- **Breadth-First Search (BFS):** In graph algorithms like BFS, queues are used to explore neighboring nodes level by level. The nodes are added to the queue in a FIFO manner.
- **Print Job Management:** Printers use queues to manage print jobs. The first document added to the queue is the first one to be printed.
- **Resource Sharing:** Queues are used to manage shared resources among multiple clients. For example, a network router may use a queue to handle incoming data packets.
- **Task Execution:** In multithreading and concurrent programming, queues are used to communicate and synchronize tasks between threads or processes.
- **Buffering:** Queues are employed in buffering scenarios where data is produced at one rate and consumed at another. This helps in handling data flow mismatches.
- **Request Handling:** Web servers and application servers use queues to manage incoming client requests. Each request is processed in the order it was received.

Implementing Queues in C

Queues are a fundamental data structure that can be efficiently implemented in the C programming language. To create a queue in C, you can use an array or a linked list as the underlying data structure.

Array-Based Queue Implementation

An array-based queue is a simple and efficient way to implement a queue in C. Here's a step-by-step guide to creating an array-based queue:

- **Define the Queue Size:** Determine the maximum number of elements the queue can hold and declare an array of that size. For example, to create a queue that can hold integers, you can use:

```
#define MAX_SIZE 100
int queue[MAX_SIZE];
```

```
int front = -1; // Initialize the front pointer
int rear = -1;  // Initialize the rear pointer
```

• **Enqueue Operation:** To enqueue (add) an element to the rear of the queue, increment the rear pointer and assign the value to the corresponding index in the array.

```
void enqueue(int value) {
   if (rear < MAX_SIZE - 1) {
      if (front == -1) {
         front = 0; // If the queue was empty, update the front pointer
      }
      queue[++rear] = value;
   } else {
      printf("Queue overflow: Cannot enqueue element %d\n", value);
   }
}
```

• **Dequeue Operation:** To dequeue (remove) an element from the front of the queue, return the element at the current front index and then increment the front pointer.

```
int dequeue() {
   if (front <= rear) {
      return queue[front++];
   } else {
      printf("Queue underflow: Queue is empty\n");
      return -1; // You can choose to return a specific value to indicate an empty queue.
   }
}
```

• **Peek Operation:** To peek at the front element without removing it, simply return the element at the current front index.

```
int peek() {
   if (front <= rear) {
      return queue[front];
   } else {
      printf("Queue is empty\n");
      return -1; // You can choose to return a specific value to indicate an empty queue.
   }
}
```

• **isEmpty Operation:** You can check if the queue is empty by examining the values of front and rear.

```
   int isEmpty() {
      return front > rear;
   }
```

Linked-List-Based Queue Implementation

A linked-list-based queue offers dynamic memory allocation and can handle a variable number of elements. Here's how to implement a linked-list-based queue:

1. **Define a Node Structure:** Start by defining a structure for the nodes in the linked list. Each node should contain the data and a pointer to the next node.

```c
struct Node {
    int data;
    struct Node* next;
};
```

- **Initialize the Queue:** Declare pointers to the front and rear of the queue and initialize them to NULL to indicate an empty queue.

```c
struct Node* front = NULL;
struct Node* rear = NULL;
```

- **Enqueue Operation:** To enqueue (add) an element to the rear of the queue, allocate memory for a new node, assign the value, and update the next pointer of the rear node to point to the new node. Then, update the rear pointer to the new node.

```c
void enqueue(int value) {
    struct Node* newNode = (struct Node*)malloc(sizeof(struct Node));
    if (newNode == NULL) {
        printf("Memory allocation failed\n");
        return;
    }
    newNode->data = value;
    newNode->next = NULL;
    if (rear == NULL) {
        front = newNode; // If the queue was empty, update the front pointer
    } else {
        rear->next = newNode;
    }
    rear = newNode;
}
```

- **Dequeue Operation:** To dequeue (remove) an element from the front of the queue, first check if the queue is empty. If not, remove the front node, free its memory, and update the front pointer to the next node.

```c
int dequeue() {
    if (isEmpty()) {
        printf("Queue is empty\n");
        return -1; // You can choose to return a specific value to indicate an empty queue.
    }
    struct Node* temp = front;
```

```
    int value = temp->data;
    front = front->next;
    free(temp);
    if (front == NULL) {
        rear = NULL; // If the queue is now empty, update the rear pointer
    }
    return value;
}
```

- **Peek Operation:** To peek at the front element without removing it, simply return the data in the front node.

```
int peek() {
    if (isEmpty()) {
        printf("Queue is empty\n");
        return -1; // You can choose to return a specific value to indicate an empty queue.
    }
    return front->data;
}
```

- **isEmpty Operation:** You can check if the queue is empty by examining the values of front and rear.

```
    int isEmpty() {
        return front == NULL;
    }
```

Choosing Between Array-Based and Linked-List-Based Queues

The choice between an array-based and a linked-list-based queue depends on your specific requirements. Here are some factors to consider:

- **Memory Usage:** Array-based queues allocate memory upfront, while linked-list-based queues allocate memory dynamically as needed. If memory usage is a concern, a linked list might be more efficient.
- **Maximum Capacity:** Array-based queues have a maximum capacity defined by the array size, while linked-list-based queues can grow dynamically. If you need a queue with a flexible size, a linked list is a better choice.
- **Insertion/Deletion Efficiency:** Array-based queues are typically more efficient for small to medium-sized queues due to constant-time insertions and deletions. Linked-list-based queues have a constant-time enqueue operation but may involve memory allocation and deallocation, which can introduce overhead.
- **Ease of Implementation:** Array-based queues are relatively straightforward to implement, while linked-list-based queues involve more complex memory management.

- **Error Handling:** Array-based queues can run into overflow errors if the queue size exceeds the predefined capacity. Linked-list-based queues can run into memory allocation errors if the system is out of memory.

Queue Applications

Queues, with their First-In, First-Out (FIFO) behavior, serve as fundamental tools in computer science and programming. They are applied across various domains to address problems efficiently and maintain a structured order of data.

1. Task Scheduling

Queues are integral to task scheduling in operating systems and multitasking environments. Processes or tasks that need to be executed are placed in a queue, and the operating system uses scheduling algorithms to determine which task to execute next based on priority, time-sharing, or other criteria.

2. Breadth-First Search (BFS)

In graph algorithms like BFS, queues are used to explore neighboring nodes level by level. Starting from the source node, BFS explores all nodes at a given depth before moving on to nodes at the next depth. This approach ensures that nodes are visited in their order of proximity to the source.

3. Print Job Management

Printers use queues to manage print jobs submitted by users or devices. Each print job is added to a queue, and the printer processes them in the order they were received. This ensures fairness in sharing the printing resource.

4. Request Handling

Web servers, application servers, and other networked systems use queues to manage incoming client requests. The requests are placed in a queue, and the server processes them sequentially, preventing overload and ensuring that each request is handled.

5. Buffering

Queues are employed in scenarios where data is produced at one rate and consumed at another. For instance, in multimedia streaming applications, data packets are enqueued as they arrive, and the consumer dequeues and plays them. This buffering mechanism smooths out data flow mismatches.

6. Task Management in Multithreading

In multithreaded programming, queues are used to communicate and synchronize tasks between threads or processes. A producer thread enqueues tasks, and one or more consumer threads dequeue and execute them. This ensures thread safety and efficient task distribution.

7. CPU Scheduling

In real-time operating systems and multiprocessor environments, queues are used to schedule tasks for CPU execution. The tasks with the highest priority or deadlines are placed at the front of the queue, ensuring that critical tasks are executed promptly.

8. Call Center Systems

Call centers use queues to manage incoming customer calls. When all operators are busy, calls are placed in a queue, and the next available operator dequeues and handles the call. This ensures that callers are serviced in the order they dialed.

9. Data Structures

Queues are building blocks for other data structures and algorithms. They are used to implement more complex structures like priority queues, double-ended queues (dequeues), and can be instrumental in solving problems like finding the shortest path in graph algorithms.

10. Simulation and Modeling

Queues are used in simulations and modeling to represent real-world scenarios where entities wait in lines or queues. For instance, they can model traffic flow at intersections or customer wait times at a service center.

11. Task Queues in Distributed Systems

In distributed systems and cloud computing environments, task queues are used to distribute and manage tasks or jobs across multiple nodes or virtual machines. These queues ensure that tasks are processed efficiently and can be distributed to available resources.

TREES

Introduction to Trees

In the world of data structures, trees are a fundamental and versatile family of structures that provide a hierarchical way to organize and store data. Unlike linear structures such as arrays and linked lists, trees branch out into a more complex and organized arrangement, making them suitable for a wide range of applications in computer science and programming.

What is a Tree?

A **tree** is a hierarchical data structure composed of nodes connected by edges. It is similar to a real-world tree with branches and leaves, where nodes represent elements or data, and edges represent relationships between those elements. The structure of a tree follows a few key rules:

1. **Root Node:** A tree has a single root node that serves as the starting point for traversing the tree. All other nodes are descendants of the root.
2. **Nodes and Edges:** A tree consists of nodes, which store data, and edges, which connect nodes. Nodes are organized into levels, with the root at level 0, and edges establish the relationships between nodes.
3. **Parent and Child Nodes:** In a tree, a node can have zero or more child nodes. The node that connects to another node below it is called the **parent** node, while the nodes connected to it are called **child** nodes.
4. **Leaf Nodes:** Nodes with no children are called **leaf nodes** or simply leaves. They are the endpoints of the tree branches and contain data but do not connect to any other nodes.
5. **Siblings:** Nodes that share the same parent are called **siblings**. They are at the same level in the tree hierarchy.

Common Terminology

To describe trees accurately, it's essential to be familiar with some common terminology:

- **Depth:** The depth of a node is the length of the path from the root node to that node. The root node has a depth of 0, and its immediate children have a depth of 1.
- **Height:** The height of a tree is the length of the longest path from the root node to any leaf node. It represents the depth of the deepest leaf node.
- **Subtree:** A subtree is a portion of a tree that is itself a tree. It consists of a node and all its descendants, including the node itself.
- **Binary Tree:** A binary tree is a type of tree in which each node can have at most two children, known as the left child and the right child.
- **N-ary Tree:** An N-ary tree is a tree in which each node can have up to N children, where N is a positive integer.

Why Trees Matter

Trees are not only a fundamental data structure but also a concept deeply rooted in computer science and programming. They are used in a multitude of scenarios, including:

- **File System Directories:** File systems on computers are often organized in a tree-like structure, with directories (folders) and files as nodes.
- **Hierarchical Data:** Trees are ideal for representing hierarchical data such as organization charts, family trees, and menu structures in software applications.
- **Database Indexing:** Databases use tree structures, such as B-trees, to efficiently search and access records.
- **Parsing Expressions:** Trees are used in parsing expressions, as they represent the hierarchical structure of mathematical expressions, making it easier to evaluate them.
- **Decision-Making:** Decision trees are used in machine learning and artificial intelligence to model decision-making processes.

Binary Trees

A **binary tree** is a fundamental type of tree in computer science and programming. It is characterized by its hierarchical structure, where each node in the tree can have at most two children: a left child and a right child. Binary trees are versatile data structures with various applications, and they serve as the foundation for more advanced tree structures and algorithms.

Anatomy of a Binary Tree

A binary tree consists of nodes connected by edges, with the following key elements:

1. **Root Node:** The topmost node of the binary tree is called the root node. It serves as the starting point for traversing the tree.
2. **Parent Node:** Each node (except the root) has a parent node, which is the node directly above it. The parent node connects to its children nodes.
3. **Child Nodes:** A node in a binary tree can have zero, one, or two children. These children are referred to as the left child and the right child.
4. **Leaf Nodes:** Nodes that have no children are called leaf nodes or leaves. They are the endpoints of the tree's branches and contain data.
5. **Internal Nodes:** Nodes that have at least one child (either left or right) are called internal nodes. They are not leaves and are situated between the root and the leaves.

Types of Binary Trees

Binary trees come in various forms, depending on their structural properties and organization. Some common types of binary trees include:

1. **Full Binary Tree:** In a full binary tree, every node has either zero children (a leaf node) or exactly two children (a left child and a right child).
2. **Complete Binary Tree:** A complete binary tree is one in which all levels of the tree are fully filled except possibly for the last level, which is filled from left to right. This property makes complete binary trees useful in heap data structures.
3. **Perfect Binary Tree:** A perfect binary tree is a binary tree in which all internal nodes have exactly two children, and all leaf nodes are at the same level. Perfect binary trees are balanced and have a height of $\log_2(N)$, where N is the total number of nodes.
4. **Balanced Binary Tree:** A balanced binary tree is a binary tree in which the depth of the left and right subtrees of every node differ by at most one. Common balanced binary trees include AVL trees and Red-Black trees, which maintain their balance through various operations.

Binary Tree Operations

Binary trees support a range of operations, including:

- **Insertion:** Adding a new node to the binary tree by finding the appropriate location based on the node's value and the binary tree's properties.
- **Deletion:** Removing a node from the binary tree while maintaining the binary tree's structure and properties.

- **Traversal:** Exploring the binary tree to visit its nodes in a specific order. Common traversal methods include in-order, pre-order, and post-order traversal.
- **Searching:** Finding a specific node in the binary tree based on its value.
- **Finding Height:** Calculating the height or depth of the binary tree, which indicates the number of levels or layers.

Binary trees are not only fundamental data structures but also serve as building blocks for more advanced tree structures and algorithms. They are used in a wide range of applications, from organizing hierarchical data to optimizing search algorithms.

Binary Search Trees (BSTs)

A **Binary Search Tree (BST)** is a specialized type of binary tree that plays a pivotal role in computer science and programming. BSTs are designed for efficient searching, insertion, and deletion of nodes, making them a fundamental data structure for various applications.

Characteristics of Binary Search Trees

Binary Search Trees possess a unique property that distinguishes them from ordinary binary trees: the values of nodes are organized such that, for any given node:

1. All nodes in its left subtree have values less than or equal to the node's value.
2. All nodes in its right subtree have values greater than the node's value.

This property is known as the **Binary Search Tree Property**, and it enables efficient searching operations. Due to this property, the values in a BST are ordered in a way that simplifies data retrieval.

Advantages of Binary Search Trees

Binary Search Trees offer several advantages:

1. **Efficient Searching:** The Binary Search Tree Property allows for fast searching operations. When searching for a value, the tree can be traversed in a logarithmic time complexity, making it efficient for large datasets.
2. **Efficient Insertion and Deletion:** Adding or removing nodes in a BST while maintaining its property is efficient. The tree's structure adapts dynamically to changes.

3. **Ordered Data:** BSTs naturally maintain data in sorted order, making it easy to retrieve data in ascending or descending order when needed.
4. **Versatility:** BSTs are versatile and can be used in various applications, including databases, search engines, and certain graph algorithms.

Operations on Binary Search Trees

BSTs support a range of operations:

1. **Insertion:** To insert a new value into a BST, it is compared to the values of existing nodes, and a suitable location is found following the BST property. The new node is then added as a leaf.
2. **Deletion:** Removing a node from a BST involves a few cases depending on whether the node has zero, one, or two children. The BST property must be maintained during the deletion process.
3. **Searching:** Searching for a specific value in a BST starts at the root and traverses the tree by comparing the value with the nodes' values, moving left or right based on the comparison until the value is found or determined to be absent.
4. **Traversal:** BSTs can be traversed in various orders:
    o **In-Order:** Visit left subtree, then the current node, then right subtree. This produces a sorted list of values.
    o **Pre-Order:** Visit the current node, then the left subtree, then the right subtree.
    o **Post-Order:** Visit the left subtree, then the right subtree, then the current node.

Balancing Binary Search Trees

While BSTs offer excellent search and insertion efficiency, their performance can degrade in the worst-case scenario when the tree becomes highly unbalanced. To maintain efficient operations, self-balancing binary search trees like AVL trees and Red-Black trees are used. These trees automatically adjust their structure to ensure a balanced height, guaranteeing logarithmic time complexity for search, insert, and delete operations.

AVL Trees: Self-Balancing Binary Search Trees

AVL Trees, named after their inventors Adelson-Velsky and Landis, are a type of self-balancing binary search tree. They were designed to address one of the primary concerns with standard binary search trees (BSTs) - maintaining a balanced structure, which ensures efficient searching, insertion, and deletion operations.

The Need for Balance

In a standard binary search tree, the efficiency of searching, inserting, or deleting nodes depends heavily on the tree's structure. If the tree becomes unbalanced, it can devolve into a linked list, causing search operations to degrade from logarithmic time complexity (O(log n)) to linear time complexity (O(n)). This loss of balance is a significant issue in real-world applications.

AVL Tree Properties

AVL trees mitigate this issue by enforcing a crucial property:

Balancing Property: For every node in an AVL tree, the heights of its left and right subtrees (known as the balance factor) differ by at most one.

In other words, the tree is always approximately balanced, ensuring that the longest path from the root to any leaf is no more than one level longer than the shortest path. This guarantees logarithmic time complexity for search, insert, and delete operations.

Balancing AVL Trees

Maintaining the balancing property is the key to AVL trees. When you insert or delete a node in an AVL tree, it may become unbalanced. In such cases, AVL trees use rotations to restore balance. There are four types of rotations:

1. **Single Left Rotation:** Used when the right subtree of a node becomes too tall compared to the left subtree.
2. **Single Right Rotation:** Used when the left subtree of a node becomes too tall compared to the right subtree.
3. **Double Left-Right Rotation:** Combines a left rotation followed by a right rotation, used when the right subtree of a node has an imbalance with its left child.
4. **Double Right-Left Rotation:** Combines a right rotation followed by a left rotation, used when the left subtree of a node has an imbalance with its right child.

By performing these rotations as needed during insertion and deletion operations, AVL trees ensure that the balancing property is maintained at all times. This prevents the tree from degenerating into an inefficient linked list structure.

Performance of AVL Trees

AVL trees guarantee logarithmic time complexity (O(log n)) for searching, inserting, and deleting nodes, even in the worst-case scenario. This makes them highly efficient and reliable for various applications where balance is crucial, such as databases, compilers, and data structures like sets and maps.

However, AVL trees come with a slight overhead due to the need for balance maintenance. This makes them slightly slower than non-balancing binary search trees for certain operations. Nevertheless, the reliability and consistent performance they offer in real-world scenarios often outweigh this overhead.

Tree Traversal Algorithms

Tree traversal refers to the process of visiting all nodes in a tree data structure systematically. Trees are hierarchical structures, and traversing them efficiently is essential for various applications, from searching and sorting to evaluating mathematical expressions and exploring hierarchical data.

In-Order Traversal

In-order traversal is a depth-first traversal algorithm that follows the left-subtree, current node, right-subtree order. In other words, when performing in-order traversal, you visit nodes in ascending order for a binary search tree (BST). Here's how it works:

1. Traverse the left subtree (recursively).
2. Visit the current node.
3. Traverse the right subtree (recursively).

In the context of a BST, in-order traversal produces a sorted list of the tree's values. It's commonly used for tasks like printing values in ascending order, checking if a tree is a valid BST, or evaluating mathematical expressions in infix notation.

Pre-Order Traversal

Pre-order traversal is another depth-first traversal algorithm that follows the current node, left-subtree, right-subtree order. Here's how it works:

1. Visit the current node.
2. Traverse the left subtree (recursively).
3. Traverse the right subtree (recursively).

Pre-order traversal is often used for tasks like creating a copy of a tree, serializing a tree for storage or communication, and constructing an expression tree from a prefix notation expression.

Post-Order Traversal

Post-order traversal is the final depth-first traversal algorithm, following the left-subtree, right-subtree, current node order. Here's how it works:

1. Traverse the left subtree (recursively).
2. Traverse the right subtree (recursively).
3. Visit the current node.

Post-order traversal is useful for tasks like deleting nodes in a tree, evaluating expressions in postfix (reverse Polish) notation, and certain graph algorithms like finding the post-order traversal of a directed acyclic graph.

Depth-First vs. Breadth-First Traversal

Depth-first traversal explores a tree as deeply as possible along a branch before backtracking to other branches. In contrast, breadth-first traversal explores all nodes at the current depth level before moving to the next level. Both traversal strategies have their uses. Depth-first traversal is often employed for tasks like searching and pathfinding, while breadth-first traversal is ideal for tasks like level-order traversal and shortest path problems.

Choosing the Right Traversal

The choice of traversal algorithm depends on the specific problem or task at hand. Each traversal order provides a unique perspective on the tree's structure and can be applied to various applications.

Tree Applications

Trees are versatile data structures with a wide range of applications in computer science and programming. Their hierarchical and organized nature makes them valuable for solving various problems.

1. Directory Structures

One of the most straightforward applications of trees is in representing directory structures in file systems. Each directory can be viewed as a node, and subdirectories and files within it as its children. This hierarchical representation allows for efficient navigation and management of files and folders.

2. XML and HTML Parsing

In web development and data interchange, trees are used to parse and represent XML and HTML documents. Parsing these documents generates a tree structure known as the Document Object Model (DOM), which is used to manipulate and interact with web content.

3. Database Indexing

Tree structures, such as B-trees and B+ trees, are widely used in database systems for indexing and organizing data. They enable fast retrieval, insertion, and deletion of records in databases, making them crucial for database performance.

4. Hierarchical Data

Trees are an intuitive choice for representing hierarchical data. They are used in organizational charts, family trees, and category hierarchies in e-commerce websites. Representing hierarchical data as trees simplifies navigation and querying.

5. Expression Parsing

In compilers and interpreters, trees are employed to parse and evaluate mathematical expressions. Expression trees represent the hierarchical structure of expressions, making it easier to perform operations like evaluation, optimization, and code generation.

6. File Compression

Huffman coding, a tree-based compression algorithm, is used to create variable-length codes for characters based on their frequencies in a text. This approach efficiently compresses files and is used in many compression utilities.

7. Network Routing

Trees play a role in computer network routing algorithms, such as spanning trees used to establish efficient routes in network topologies. Spanning trees ensure connectivity while avoiding cycles in a network.

8. Game Trees

In artificial intelligence and game theory, trees are used to model decision-making processes in games. Minimax and alpha-beta pruning algorithms work with game trees to determine optimal moves in games like chess and tic-tac-toe.

9. Syntax Trees

In programming languages and compilers, syntax trees (also known as abstract syntax trees) are used to represent the hierarchical structure of code. These trees facilitate parsing, code analysis, optimization, and code generation.

10. Machine Learning

Decision trees are used in machine learning for classification and regression tasks. These trees help in making decisions based on input features, making them interpretable models for various applications.

11. Robotics and Robotics Path Planning

In robotics, trees are used for path planning and navigation. Algorithms like Rapidly-exploring Random Trees (RRTs) are employed to plan feasible paths for robots in complex environments.

12. Data Compression

Wavelet trees and trie structures are used in data compression and pattern matching algorithms. They enable efficient storage and retrieval of compressed data.

These are just a few examples of the many applications of trees in computer science and programming. Trees provide an organized and efficient way to represent, store, and manipulate hierarchical data and have a profound impact on problem-solving and data management across diverse domains.

HEAPS AND PRIORITY QUEUES

Introduction to Heaps

Heaps are a class of specialized tree-based structures designed for efficient retrieval and management of priority-based data. They are particularly valuable when you need to quickly access the most significant or least significant element in a dataset. Heaps are the foundation of priority queues, a critical concept in computer science and various applications.

What is a Heap?

A **heap** is a complete binary tree that satisfies the **heap property**, which differs slightly between two common types of heaps: **max-heap** and **min-heap**.

- **Max-Heap:** In a max-heap, for any given node I, the value of I is greater than or equal to the values of its children nodes. This means that the highest priority element (maximum value) is at the root of the tree.
- **Min-Heap:** In a min-heap, for any given node I, the value of I is less than or equal to the values of its children nodes. This ensures that the lowest priority element (minimum value) is at the root.

The shape of a heap is usually a complete binary tree, meaning that all levels of the tree are fully filled except possibly for the last level, which is filled from left to right. This ensures efficient memory usage and a balanced structure.

Why Heaps Matter

Heaps are designed to provide efficient access to the most significant or least significant element (depending on whether it's a max-heap or min-heap) in a dataset. This priority-based organization is invaluable in various real-world scenarios:

1. **Priority Queues:** Priority queues, built on top of heaps, are used in algorithms and systems where elements need to be processed based on their priority or importance. Examples include task scheduling in operating systems and shortest path algorithms.
2. **Heap Sort:** Heap sort is an efficient in-place sorting algorithm that relies on heaps to rearrange elements in ascending or descending order.
3. **Graph Algorithms:** In algorithms like Dijkstra's algorithm and Prim's algorithm for Minimum Spanning Trees, heaps help efficiently select and process the next element.
4. **Efficient Retrieval:** Heaps are useful for maintaining collections of data where you need quick access to the most significant or least significant element, such as finding the kth largest or smallest element.
5. **Data Compression:** Huffman coding, a widely used data compression algorithm, relies on heaps to construct efficient variable-length codes for characters based on their frequencies.

Heap Operations

Heaps support several fundamental operations, including:

- **Insertion:** Adding a new element to the heap while maintaining the heap property.
- **Deletion:** Removing the most significant or least significant element (depending on the type of heap) and restoring the heap property.
- **Peek:** Accessing the most significant or least significant element without removing it.
- **Heapify:** Converting an array of elements into a heap structure efficiently.

Types of Heaps

While the classic binary heap is widely used, other specialized heaps like binomial heaps and Fibonacci heaps offer different trade-offs in terms of time complexity for specific operations. Each type of heap has its strengths and weaknesses, making them suitable for different scenarios.

Binary Heaps

Binary heaps are a fundamental type of heap data structure, designed to efficiently implement priority queues and solve problems where elements need to be processed based on their priority. Binary heaps are known for their simplicity and excellent performance in terms of insertion, deletion, and retrieval of the most significant or least significant element, depending on whether they are max-heaps or min-heaps.

Characteristics of Binary Heaps

Binary heaps are characterized by the following properties:

1. **Binary Tree Structure:** A binary heap is a complete binary tree, which means all levels are fully filled except possibly for the last level, which is filled from left to right. This structural property ensures efficient memory usage.
2. **Heap Property:** Binary heaps adhere to the heap property, which varies between max-heaps and min-heaps:
    o **Max-Heap Property:** In a max-heap, for any given node I, the value of I is greater than or equal to the values of its children nodes. This property ensures that the maximum element is at the root.
    o **Min-Heap Property:** In a min-heap, for any given node I, the value of I is less than or equal to the values of its children nodes. This property ensures that the minimum element is at the root.
3. **Efficient Retrieval:** Retrieving the most significant or least significant element in a binary heap (the root) takes constant time, O(1).

Common Operations on Binary Heaps

Binary heaps support several key operations:

1. **Insertion:** Adding a new element to the heap while maintaining the heap property. This typically involves "bubbling up" the newly inserted element to its appropriate position in the tree.
2. **Deletion:** Removing the root element from the heap while preserving the heap property. After removal, the last element in the heap usually replaces the root, and it may need to "bubble down" to its correct position.
3. **Peek:** Accessing the most significant or least significant element (the root) without removing it. This operation is particularly useful when you want to examine the priority element without altering the heap's state.
4. **Heapify:** Constructing a binary heap from an unordered array efficiently. The heapify operation ensures that the binary heap property is satisfied for all nodes.

Applications of Binary Heaps

Binary heaps find applications in various scenarios:

1. **Priority Queues:** Binary heaps are commonly used as the underlying data structure for priority queues, where elements are processed based on their priority.
2. **Heap Sort:** The heap sort algorithm, which leverages binary heaps, efficiently sorts an array in ascending or descending order.
3. **Graph Algorithms:** Algorithms like Dijkstra's shortest path algorithm and Prim's minimum spanning tree algorithm use binary heaps for efficient selection and processing of nodes.
4. **Job Scheduling:** In operating systems, binary heaps can be used to manage the scheduling of processes or tasks based on their priority levels.
5. **Efficient Selection:** Binary heaps enable efficient selection of the kth largest or smallest element from an array.

Priority Queues

Priority queues are abstract data types that build on the concept of heaps and are designed to efficiently manage elements based on their priority or importance. They enable the retrieval and processing of the most significant or least significant element quickly, making them invaluable in various applications where tasks or data must be ordered by importance.

What is a Priority Queue?

A **priority queue** is a data structure that maintains a collection of elements, each associated with a priority value. The key feature of a priority queue is that it allows efficient access to the element with the highest (in a max-priority queue) or lowest (in a min-priority queue) priority. Priority queues are often used to manage tasks or events that need to be processed in a specific order.

Priority Queue Properties

Priority queues exhibit the following properties:

1. **Element-Priority Association:** Each element in the priority queue is associated with a priority value, which determines its position within the queue.
2. **Efficient Access:** The priority queue provides efficient access to the element with the highest or lowest priority, typically in constant time (O(1)).

3. **Insertion and Deletion:** Elements can be efficiently inserted into and removed from the priority queue while maintaining the order based on their priority. These operations usually take logarithmic time (O(log n)).
4. **No Particular Order:** While elements within the priority queue have priorities, there is no inherent order among elements with the same priority. The order of elements with equal priority is not guaranteed.

Operations on Priority Queues

Priority queues support several fundamental operations:

1. **Insertion:** Adding an element with an associated priority to the priority queue.
2. **Deletion:** Removing the element with the highest (in a max-priority queue) or lowest (in a min-priority queue) priority from the priority queue.
3. **Peek:** Accessing the element with the highest or lowest priority without removing it.

Implementation of Priority Queues

Priority queues can be implemented using various data structures, with binary heaps being a popular choice due to their efficiency. Depending on the application, other data structures such as Fibonacci heaps and binomial heaps may be preferred for their specific characteristics.

Real-World Applications

Priority queues find applications in a wide range of real-world scenarios:

1. **Operating Systems:** Task scheduling in operating systems often involves priority queues to determine which process or task to execute next based on its priority.
2. **Dijkstra's Algorithm:** In graph algorithms like Dijkstra's shortest path algorithm, a priority queue helps select and process nodes efficiently based on their distances from the source node.
3. **Network Routing:** Priority queues are used in network routing protocols to prioritize and route packets efficiently.
4. **Simulation:** In simulations, such as event-driven simulations, priority queues help manage and process events based on their occurrence time.
5. **Emergency Services:** Emergency services use priority queues to manage and dispatch emergency calls based on their severity.
6. **Data Compression:** Huffman coding, a data compression technique, uses priority queues to construct optimal variable-length codes for characters based on their frequencies.

Heap Sort Algorithm

Heap sort is a highly efficient in-place sorting algorithm that leverages the structure and properties of binary heaps to rearrange elements in an array. It is known for its stability, predictable performance characteristics, and adaptability to various data types.

Overview of Heap Sort

Heap sort is a comparison-based sorting algorithm that divides the input array into two parts: a sorted region and an unsorted region. The algorithm repeatedly extracts the maximum (in a max-heap) or minimum (in a min-heap) element from the unsorted region and adds it to the sorted region. This process continues until the entire array is sorted.

Heapify: Building a Heap

Before we can perform heap sort, we need to convert the input array into a valid heap. This operation, called **heapify**, ensures that the heap property is satisfied for all nodes in the tree. Heapify is typically performed in two phases:

1. **Build Phase:** In this phase, we start from the last non-leaf node and "heapify down" each node towards the root of the tree. This guarantees that the largest (in a max-heap) or smallest (in a min-heap) element ends up at the root.
2. **Sort Phase:** After the heap is built, we repeatedly extract the root element, swap it with the last element in the unsorted region, reduce the size of the unsorted region, and perform a "heapify down" operation on the root to maintain the heap property. This process continues until the entire array is sorted.

Heap Sort Time Complexity

Heap sort has several attractive features in terms of time complexity:

- **Worst-Case and Average-Case Time Complexity:** Heap sort guarantees a consistent O(n log n) time complexity for both worst-case and average-case scenarios.
- **In-Place Sorting:** Heap sort sorts the input array in-place, meaning it doesn't require additional memory for auxiliary data structures. This property is particularly beneficial when sorting large datasets.

- **Stable Sort:** Heap sort is a stable sorting algorithm, which means it maintains the relative order of equal elements in the sorted output.

Advantages and Disadvantages

Heap sort offers the following advantages:

- **Predictable Performance:** Heap sort consistently performs in O(n log n) time, making it suitable for large datasets.
- **In-Place Sorting:** Its in-place sorting nature ensures efficient memory usage.

However, heap sort also has some drawbacks:

- **Lack of Adaptive Behavior:** Unlike some other sorting algorithms like quicksort, heap sort does not adapt to the existing order of elements. It consistently performs in O(n log n) time, even if the input is partially sorted.
- **Slower for Small Datasets:** For small datasets, the overhead of heapify and the heap maintenance steps can make heap sort less efficient than simpler algorithms like insertion sort.

HASHING

Introduction to Hashing

Hashing is a fundamental technique that provides a way to efficiently store, search, and retrieve data. At its core, hashing involves taking an input (or 'key') and using a hash function to transform it into a fixed-size string of characters, typically a hash code or hash value. This hash code is then used as an index to access or store the associated data in a data structure called a hash table.

The Essence of Hashing

At its essence, hashing can be likened to assigning a unique address to every piece of data you want to store. Imagine a library that uses a unique code for each book, allowing you to quickly locate a book on the shelf based on its code. Hashing serves a similar purpose in the digital world.

Key Concepts in Hashing

Here are some key concepts that form the foundation of hashing:

1. **Hash Function:** A **hash function** is a mathematical algorithm that takes an input (or 'key') and produces a fixed-size string of characters, which is typically a hash code. The hash function ensures that the same input will always produce the same hash code.
2. **Hash Code:** The output of a hash function is called a **hash code** or **hash value**. It is a unique identifier for the input data. Hash codes are typically integers or fixed-length strings of characters.

3. **Hash Table:** A **hash table** is a data structure that uses hash codes as indices to store and retrieve data. It provides efficient insertion, deletion, and retrieval operations.

The Role of Hashing

Hashing plays a crucial role in various aspects of computer science and data management:

1. **Data Retrieval:** Hashing allows for rapid data retrieval. Instead of searching through a large dataset item by item, you can compute the hash code of the item you're looking for and directly access it in the hash table.
2. **Data Storage:** Hashing provides an efficient way to store data. Data is organized based on its hash code, allowing for quick and organized storage.
3. **Caching:** In caching systems, hashing helps identify whether a requested item is already in the cache. This speeds up access times and reduces the need to fetch data from slower storage mediums.
4. **Data Integrity:** Hashing is used to verify the integrity of data during transmission. By comparing hash codes before and after transmission, you can detect any changes or corruption in the data.
5. **Password Storage:** Hashing is essential for securely storing passwords. Instead of storing plaintext passwords, systems store the hash codes of passwords. During authentication, the system hashes the entered password and checks if it matches the stored hash.

Real-World Applications

Hashing is used in a multitude of real-world applications, including database indexing, file systems, password security, data deduplication, and more. It is a fundamental concept in computer science and plays a vital role in optimizing data access and storage.

Hash Functions

These mathematical algorithms take input data and convert it into a fixed-size string of characters, known as a hash code or hash value. The resulting hash code serves as a unique identifier for the input data and is crucial for efficient data retrieval, storage, and security.

The Anatomy of a Hash Function

A hash function takes an input, typically of arbitrary size, and produces a fixed-size output, which is a hash code. The characteristics of a good hash function include:

1. **Deterministic:** For the same input, a hash function must consistently produce the same hash code. This property ensures predictability and reliability.
2. **Efficient:** Hash functions should be computationally efficient, allowing for quick computation of hash codes.
3. **Fixed Output Size:** Hash functions generate hash codes of a fixed length, regardless of the input size. This property ensures uniformity in storage and indexing.
4. **Avalanche Effect:** A small change in the input should result in a significantly different hash code. This property makes hash codes resistant to collisions and ensures that similar inputs have distinct hash codes.
5. **Pre-image Resistance:** Given a hash code, it should be computationally infeasible to determine the original input. This property is crucial for password security.
6. **Collision Resistance:** It should be unlikely that two different inputs produce the same hash code. Collision resistance is vital for maintaining data integrity.

Use Cases of Hash Functions

Hash functions find applications in various domains:

1. **Data Retrieval:** Hash functions are used in hash tables to enable rapid data retrieval. Given a key, the hash function produces an index that points directly to the location of the associated data.
2. **Data Integrity:** Hash functions are employed to verify the integrity of data during transmission. By comparing the hash code of received data with the expected hash code, errors or tampering can be detected.
3. **Password Security:** In password storage, plaintext passwords are not stored directly. Instead, their hash codes are stored. During authentication, the entered password is hashed and compared to the stored hash code.
4. **Digital Signatures:** Hash functions are a crucial component of digital signatures, ensuring the authenticity and integrity of digitally signed documents.
5. **Cryptography:** Hash functions are used in cryptographic algorithms for data integrity verification, message authentication codes (MACs), and more.

Several well-known hash functions are widely used in practice, including:

1. **MD5 (Message Digest 5):** Despite its historical significance, MD5 is no longer considered secure due to vulnerabilities.
2. **SHA-1 (Secure Hash Algorithm 1):** Similar to MD5, SHA-1 is deprecated for security-critical applications due to vulnerabilities.
3. **SHA-256 (and other SHA-2 variants):** Part of the SHA-2 family, SHA-256 is widely used in secure communications, digital signatures, and more.
4. **SHA-3:** The latest member of the Secure Hash Algorithm family, designed to provide a high level of security.

Hash Tables

These data structures, often referred to as hash maps or associative arrays, enable rapid storage and retrieval of data by leveraging the power of hash functions. Hash tables are essential in a wide range of applications, from optimizing database queries to implementing dictionaries and caches.

The Anatomy of a Hash Table

A hash table is a data structure that uses a combination of a **hash function** and an array to store data. Here's how it works:

1. **Hash Function:** Each piece of data (often referred to as a "key") is processed by a hash function, which generates a unique index (or "hash code") for that key. This index determines where the data will be stored in the array.
2. **Array:** The hash table consists of an array with a fixed number of slots or buckets. Each slot can store one piece of data or multiple pieces in the form of key-value pairs.
3. **Data Storage:** When data is inserted into the hash table, it is assigned a hash code by the hash function, and the data is placed in the corresponding slot (bucket) in the array.
4. **Data Retrieval:** To retrieve data, the hash function is applied to the key to find the corresponding slot in the array, allowing for quick access to the stored data.

Advantages of Hash Tables

Hash tables offer several key advantages:

1. **Rapid Data Retrieval:** Hash tables provide constant-time (O(1)) average-case access to data. This means that regardless of the size of the dataset, data retrieval is nearly instantaneous.
2. **Efficient Data Storage:** Hash tables efficiently store data without requiring contiguous memory blocks. This property makes them suitable for dynamic and unpredictable workloads.
3. **Dynamic Sizing:** Many hash table implementations support dynamic resizing, allowing the table to grow or shrink as needed to maintain efficiency.
4. **Versatility:** Hash tables are versatile and can be used for various applications, including dictionary data structures, caches, and optimizing database queries.

Collision Resolution

While hash tables are efficient, they are not immune to a phenomenon called **collision**, which occurs when two different keys produce the same hash code. Collision resolution strategies are used to address this issue. Common collision resolution methods include:

1. **Separate Chaining:** Each slot in the array contains a linked list or other data structure to handle multiple items that hash to the same index.
2. **Open Addressing:** When a collision occurs, open addressing searches for the next available slot in the array, typically using techniques like linear probing or quadratic probing.
3. **Double Hashing:** This method uses a secondary hash function to determine the next slot to search for when a collision occurs.

Real-World Applications

Hash tables are widely used in various real-world scenarios, including:

1. **Databases:** Hash tables are employed in database systems to optimize query performance by indexing data.
2. **Caching:** Caches in systems such as web servers and browsers use hash tables to store frequently accessed data for faster retrieval.
3. **Dictionaries:** Programming languages and software libraries often implement dictionaries using hash tables for efficient key-value storage.
4. **Password Storage:** Securely storing passwords using hash tables ensures that plaintext passwords are not stored, enhancing security.

Collision Resolution Techniques

Collisions occur when two or more distinct keys produce the same hash code, leading to conflicts in data storage and retrieval. To address collisions and maintain the integrity and efficiency of hash tables, various collision resolution techniques are employed.

1. Separate Chaining

Separate chaining is one of the most straightforward collision resolution techniques. Instead of storing data directly in the hash table slots, each slot contains a data structure, typically a linked list, that can hold multiple key-value pairs with the same hash code. When a collision occurs, the new key-value pair is appended to the appropriate linked list.

- **Advantages:** Separate chaining is simple to implement and handles collisions well, even when they are frequent. It also allows for dynamic sizing of the hash table.
- **Disadvantages:** It may lead to inefficient memory usage and potentially slow performance when the linked lists become long. In the worst case, the time complexity for data retrieval can degrade to O(n), where n is the number of elements in a particular slot's linked list.

2. Open Addressing

Open addressing is a collision resolution technique that stores multiple items in the same slot but within the main array. When a collision occurs, open addressing searches for the next available slot in the array and stores the item there. This process continues until an empty slot is found.

- **Linear Probing:** In linear probing, the search for the next slot is done linearly, i.e., slot by slot. If a collision occurs at slot i, the algorithm searches slot i+1, i+2, and so on until an empty slot is found.
- **Quadratic Probing:** Quadratic probing uses a quadratic function to determine the next slot to search for when a collision occurs. It typically follows a sequence like i^2, (i+1)^2, (i+2)^2, and so on.
- **Double Hashing:** Double hashing employs a secondary hash function to calculate the interval between slots when resolving collisions. It offers more uniform distribution of items.
- **Advantages:** Open addressing avoids the need for additional data structures like linked lists, which can lead to better cache performance. It's suitable for scenarios where memory usage must be minimized.
- **Disadvantages:** Clustering can occur in open addressing, where slots closer to a collision point become densely populated, leading to slower

performance. Additionally, open addressing can be less efficient when the hash table is nearly full.

3. Robin Hood Hashing

Robin Hood hashing is a variation of open addressing that aims to reduce clustering and provide more equitable distribution of items in the hash table. When a collision occurs, Robin Hood hashing compares the distance between the current slot and the desired slot for the new item. If the new item is closer to its desired slot than the existing item, it swaps them. This process continues until the new item finds a suitable slot or the probing distance exceeds a certain threshold.

- **Advantages:** Robin Hood hashing can lead to more balanced distributions and less clustering compared to traditional open addressing techniques.
- **Disadvantages:** It may require more complex logic for item reordering, and its performance can degrade if the threshold value is not chosen carefully.

Hashing Applications

Hashing is a versatile and fundamental concept in computer science, with applications spanning a wide range of domains. Its ability to transform data into fixed-size representations and ensure efficient data retrieval, integrity verification, and security makes it indispensable in various real-world scenarios.

1. Data Retrieval and Indexing

One of the primary applications of hashing is in data retrieval and indexing. Hash tables are extensively used to organize and manage large datasets efficiently. By employing hash functions, data can be quickly stored and retrieved, making hash tables ideal for optimizing database queries, dictionary data structures, and caching systems.

2. Caching

Caches are temporary storage areas that store frequently accessed data to speed up subsequent access. Hashing is vital in cache management, as it enables quick lookup of cached items. Web browsers, content delivery networks (CDNs), and various software applications use caching to reduce latency and enhance user experiences.

3. Data Deduplication

In storage systems, data deduplication is the process of identifying and eliminating duplicate copies of data. Hash functions help identify duplicate data by generating hash codes for each data block. Identical hash codes indicate duplicate data, allowing for efficient deduplication and storage space savings.

4. Password Storage and Authentication

Hashing plays a pivotal role in enhancing security, particularly in password storage and authentication systems. Instead of storing plaintext passwords, systems store their hash codes. During authentication, the user-provided password is hashed and compared to the stored hash code. This way, even if the hash code is compromised, attackers cannot easily retrieve the original password.

5. Digital Signatures

Digital signatures use hash functions to ensure the authenticity and integrity of digitally signed documents or messages. A hash code of the message is generated, and this hash code is encrypted using a private key to create the digital signature. The recipient can verify the signature by decrypting it with the sender's public key and comparing it to a hash code generated from the received message.

6. Cryptographic Hash Functions

Cryptographic hash functions are designed to meet specific security requirements, such as pre-image resistance, collision resistance, and avalanche effect. They are used in cryptographic protocols, digital certificates, secure communications, and blockchain technology to ensure data integrity and prevent tampering.

7. Data Structures and Algorithms

Hashing is an essential component of various data structures and algorithms. Hash functions are used in hash tables, bloom filters, and hash-based data structures like hash sets and hash maps. Additionally, hashing algorithms play a critical role in optimizing search algorithms and solving problems efficiently.

8. Data Integrity Verification

Hash codes are commonly used to verify the integrity of transmitted or stored data. By comparing the hash code of received data to the expected hash code, any alterations or corruption can be detected. This is crucial in ensuring data integrity during data transfers and backups.

9. Blockchain Technology

Blockchain, the technology behind cryptocurrencies like Bitcoin, relies heavily on cryptographic hash functions. Each block in a blockchain contains a hash code of the previous block, creating a chain of blocks. This cryptographic linkage ensures the immutability and integrity of the entire blockchain, making it resistant to tampering.

GRAPHS

Introduction to Graphs

In the world of data representation and analysis, **graphs** stand as one of the most versatile and expressive structures. Graphs are a fundamental concept in computer science, mathematics, and countless real-world applications. They provide a powerful way to model and understand relationships, connections, and dependencies in a variety of domains.

The Essence of Graphs

Imagine a world where entities—whether they are people, cities, web pages, or molecules—are connected by various relationships or interactions. Graphs provide a natural and intuitive way to represent and analyze these connections. At its core, a **graph** is a mathematical and abstract representation of a set of objects (nodes or vertices) and the relationships between them (edges).

Key Concepts in Graph Theory

Before delving deeper into graphs, let's establish some key concepts:

1. **Node (Vertex):** A **node**, also known as a **vertex**, represents an entity in the graph. For instance, in a social network, each person can be represented as a node.
2. **Edge:** An **edge** represents a connection or relationship between two nodes. If we consider people in a social network, an edge might represent a friendship or a follow relationship.
3. **Directed vs. Undirected:** In an **undirected graph**, edges have no direction; they simply connect nodes. In a **directed graph** (or digraph), edges have a

direction, indicating that the relationship between nodes flows in one direction.

4. **Weighted vs. Unweighted:** In a **weighted graph**, each edge has a numerical value (weight) associated with it, representing the strength, cost, or distance of the relationship. Unweighted graphs have no such values.

5. **Cycle:** A **cycle** is a path that starts and ends at the same node, passing through a sequence of nodes and edges without repeating any node (except for the start and end nodes).

Graphs in the Real World

Graphs find applications in numerous real-world scenarios:

1. **Social Networks:** Social media platforms use graphs to model friendships, connections, and interactions between users.

2. **Transportation Networks:** Road networks, flight routes, and public transportation systems are modeled as graphs to optimize route planning and logistics.

3. **Web Link Analysis:** Search engines like Google use graphs to represent web pages and their hyperlinks for ranking and indexing.

4. **Recommendation Systems:** Graph-based algorithms power recommendation engines, suggesting products, movies, or connections based on user behavior and preferences.

5. **Network Analysis:** Graph theory helps analyze and optimize computer networks, communication systems, and supply chains.

6. **Biology and Chemistry:** Graphs represent molecular structures, protein interactions, and genetic relationships, aiding research in biology and chemistry.

Representing Graphs in C

When working with graphs in C, it's essential to choose an appropriate data structure for representing the graph's nodes and edges. The choice of representation depends on the type of graph (directed or undirected), the application's requirements, and the trade-offs between memory usage and computational complexity.

1. Adjacency Matrix

The **adjacency matrix** is a straightforward way to represent a graph, especially for small to moderately sized graphs. It uses a two-dimensional array where each row and column correspond to a vertex in the graph. The value in the cell (i, j) is 1 if there is an edge between vertex i and vertex j; otherwise, it's 0 for an unweighted graph.

```
int graph[MAX_VERTICES][MAX_VERTICES];
```

- **Advantages:**
  - o It provides quick access to whether an edge exists between two vertices (O(1) time complexity).
  - o It's memory-efficient for dense graphs.
- **Disadvantages:**
  - o It consumes a lot of memory for sparse graphs.
  - o It doesn't store edge weights for weighted graphs.

2. Adjacency List

The **adjacency list** representation is more memory-efficient and versatile than the adjacency matrix. In this representation, you use an array of lists (or dynamic arrays) to store the neighbors of each vertex. Each list contains the vertices adjacent to a particular vertex.

```
typedef struct Node {
    int vertex;
    struct Node* next;
} Node;

Node* graph[MAX_VERTICES];
```

- **Advantages:**
  - o It's memory-efficient for sparse graphs.
  - o It can store edge weights and additional information for each edge.
  - o Traversing neighbors is efficient (O(degree of the vertex)).
- **Disadvantages:**
  - o Determining whether an edge exists between two vertices requires searching the adjacency list (O(degree of the vertex)).

3. Edge List

The **edge list** representation is a simple and memory-efficient way to represent a graph, especially when you only need to store the edges and their weights.

```
typedef struct Edge {
    int source;
    int destination;
    int weight;
} Edge;

Edge edges[MAX_EDGES];
```

- **Advantages:**

- o Memory-efficient for sparse graphs.
- o Ideal for algorithms like Kruskal's Minimum Spanning Tree algorithm.
- **Disadvantages:**
  - o Determining adjacency and quickly accessing neighbors can be less efficient (O(E) time complexity, where E is the number of edges).

4. Other Representations

Depending on the specific requirements of your application, you may encounter other graph representations like incidence matrices, compact representations for specialized graphs (e.g., trees, forests), or more complex data structures for specialized tasks.

Choosing the Right Representation

The choice of graph representation depends on the nature of your graph and the operations you need to perform frequently. For example, if your graph is sparse and you often need to find adjacent vertices, an adjacency list is a suitable choice. If you're working with a dense graph and need quick edge existence checks, an adjacency matrix may be more appropriate.

In practice, you may also need to consider trade-offs between memory usage and time complexity for various operations.

Graph Traversal Algorithms (DFS and BFS)

Graph traversal algorithms are essential tools for navigating and analyzing graphs. They enable you to explore the relationships and connections within a graph, uncover hidden patterns, and solve various real-world problems. Two primary graph traversal algorithms are **Depth-First Search (DFS)** and **Breadth-First Search (BFS)**.

Depth-First Search (DFS)

Depth-First Search (DFS) is a systematic algorithm for exploring a graph by traversing as far as possible along each branch before backtracking. It employs a stack or recursion to keep track of the nodes to visit, ensuring that all nodes are visited eventually. Here's how DFS works:

1. Start at a specified node (the "source" or "start" node).
2. Mark the node as visited.

3. Explore an unvisited neighbor of the current node.
4. Repeat steps 2 and 3 for the neighbor until no unvisited neighbors remain.
5. Backtrack to the previous node and explore its unvisited neighbors.
6. Repeat steps 2 to 5 until all nodes are visited.

DFS is often used to search for paths, cycles, and connected components within a graph. It can also be used in topological sorting and solving puzzles like mazes.

Breadth-First Search (BFS)

Breadth-First Search (BFS) is another graph traversal algorithm that systematically explores a graph, but it prioritizes visiting all the neighbors of a node before moving on to their neighbors. BFS uses a queue to manage the order in which nodes are visited. Here's how BFS works:

1. Start at a specified node (the "source" or "start" node).
2. Mark the node as visited and enqueue it.
3. Dequeue a node from the queue and explore its unvisited neighbors.
4. Mark each unvisited neighbor as visited and enqueue them.
5. Repeat steps 3 and 4 until the queue is empty.

BFS is often used to find the shortest path between two nodes in an unweighted graph, discover the connected components of a graph, and explore levels of nodes in a tree or hierarchy.

Comparing DFS and BFS

DFS and BFS have distinct characteristics and are suitable for different tasks:

- **DFS** is well-suited for tasks where you need to explore deeply, such as finding paths, cycles, or connected components. It is typically implemented using recursion or a stack.
- **BFS** is ideal for tasks that require exploring neighbors before moving deeper into the graph, making it excellent for finding shortest paths in unweighted graphs or discovering connected components. It is implemented using a queue.

Applications of DFS and BFS

These traversal algorithms find applications in various fields:

1. **Pathfinding:** DFS and BFS are used to find paths between nodes in maps, routing, and navigation systems.

2. **Network Analysis:** They help analyze networks, discover communities, and identify influential nodes in social networks.
3. **Web Crawling:** BFS is used in web crawling to explore and index web pages systematically.
4. **Puzzle Solving:** Both algorithms are used to solve puzzles like mazes, Sudoku, and the Eight-Puzzle.
5. **Artificial Intelligence:** DFS and BFS serve as building blocks for various AI algorithms, including search algorithms and game-playing algorithms.

Shortest Path Algorithms (Dijkstra's and Bellman-Ford)

Shortest path algorithms are fundamental tools for finding the shortest route between two nodes in a graph, considering edge weights that represent distances, costs, or other metrics. Two well-known algorithms for solving the shortest path problem are **Dijkstra's algorithm** and the **Bellman-Ford algorithm**.

Dijkstra's Algorithm

Dijkstra's algorithm is a greedy algorithm that finds the shortest path from a source node to all other nodes in a weighted, directed or undirected graph with non-negative edge weights. It maintains a priority queue (or min-heap) of nodes to visit, starting with the source node. Here's how Dijkstra's algorithm works:

1. Initialize the distance to the source node as 0 and all other distances as infinity.
2. Add the source node to the priority queue with a distance of 0.
3. While the priority queue is not empty: a. Dequeue the node with the smallest distance. b. For each neighbor of the dequeued node: i. Calculate the tentative distance from the source node to the neighbor. ii. If the tentative distance is less than the current recorded distance, update the distance. iii. Add the neighbor to the priority queue.

Dijkstra's algorithm guarantees finding the shortest paths when all edge weights are non-negative. It works efficiently for sparse graphs and provides an ordered list of nodes sorted by their distance from the source.

Bellman-Ford Algorithm

The **Bellman-Ford algorithm** is a versatile algorithm that finds the shortest path from a source node to all other nodes in a weighted, directed or undirected graph, even when negative edge weights are present. It is based on the principle of relaxation, where it iteratively updates distance estimates for nodes until convergence. Here's how the Bellman-Ford algorithm works:

1. Initialize the distance to the source node as 0 and all other distances as infinity.
2. Repeat the following step for the number of vertices minus one times (V-1 times), where V is the number of vertices: a. For each edge (u, v) with weight w: i. Relax the edge: If the distance to v through u is shorter than the current recorded distance to v, update the distance.
3. Perform an additional iteration to check for negative-weight cycles: a. If the distance to v can still be improved through relaxation, a negative-weight cycle exists.

Bellman-Ford is a robust algorithm that can handle graphs with negative edge weights and detect negative-weight cycles. However, it is less efficient than Dijkstra's algorithm for sparse graphs and has a time complexity of $O(V*E)$, where V is the number of vertices and E is the number of edges.

Applications of Shortest Path Algorithms

Shortest path algorithms have a wide range of applications, including:

1. **Navigation Systems:** Finding the shortest route between two locations on a map.
2. **Network Routing:** Determining the most efficient path for data packets in computer networks.
3. **Flight Planning:** Optimizing flight routes for airlines to minimize fuel consumption.
4. **Robotics:** Path planning for robots to navigate environments efficiently.
5. **Game Development:** Creating realistic paths for characters in video games.
6. **Social Network Analysis:** Measuring influence or reach between users in a social network.
7. **Economic Models:** Modeling supply chain logistics and minimizing transportation costs.

Minimum Spanning Tree Algorithms (Prim's and Kruskal's)

Minimum spanning tree (MST) algorithms are essential tools for finding the smallest set of edges that connect all nodes in a connected, undirected graph. These algorithms are commonly used in network design, circuit layout, and optimization problems. Two widely recognized MST algorithms are **Prim's algorithm** and **Kruskal's algorithm.**

Prim's Algorithm

Prim's algorithm is a greedy algorithm that starts with an arbitrary node and repeatedly adds the shortest edge that connects a vertex in the MST to a vertex outside the MST. The algorithm maintains two sets of vertices: one in the MST and one outside. Here's how Prim's algorithm works:

1. Initialize the MST with a single vertex (any arbitrary vertex).
2. Repeat the following steps until all vertices are in the MST: a. Find the minimum-weight edge that connects a vertex in the MST to a vertex outside the MST. b. Add the vertex connected by the edge to the MST. c. Add the edge to the MST.

Prim's algorithm ensures that the MST remains connected and contains the minimum-weight edges that connect all vertices. It is efficient for sparse and dense graphs and can handle graphs with both positive and negative edge weights.

Kruskal's Algorithm

Kruskal's algorithm is another greedy algorithm that builds an MST by repeatedly adding the shortest edge from the set of edges not yet included in the MST. The algorithm maintains a set of disjoint subsets, each representing a connected component of the graph. Here's how Kruskal's algorithm works:

1. Initialize the MST as an empty set.
2. Sort all edges in ascending order of weight.
3. Iterate through the sorted edges: a. If adding the edge to the MST does not create a cycle, add it to the MST. b. Otherwise, discard the edge.

Kruskal's algorithm ensures that the MST remains acyclic, and it finds the minimum-weight edges that connect all vertices. It is efficient for sparse graphs and can handle graphs with both positive and negative edge weights.

Comparing Prim's and Kruskal's Algorithms

Prim's and Kruskal's algorithms share similarities as they both use a greedy approach to build MSTs. However, they have some differences:

- **Prim's algorithm** starts from a single vertex and grows the MST by adding edges that connect the MST to vertices outside. It tends to build the MST from one side.

- **Kruskal's algorithm** starts with an empty MST and adds edges one by one while ensuring that no cycles are formed. It tends to explore the graph more evenly.

The choice between these algorithms often depends on the specific problem and the characteristics of the input graph.

Applications of Minimum Spanning Trees

MST algorithms find applications in various domains, including:

1. **Network Design:** Constructing efficient communication networks with minimal cost.
2. **Circuit Design:** Laying out electronic circuits to minimize wire length.
3. **Clustering:** Grouping data points into clusters with minimal total distance.
4. **Image Segmentation:** Identifying regions of interest in medical images and computer vision.
5. **Approximation Algorithms:** Providing near-optimal solutions to complex optimization problems.

SORTING ALGORITHMS

Bubble Sort

Bubble Sort is a simple and straightforward sorting algorithm that repeatedly steps through a list of elements, compares adjacent elements, and swaps them if they are in the wrong order. This process continues until the entire list is sorted. Despite its simplicity, bubble sort is not efficient for large datasets and is mainly used for educational purposes or when simplicity is more important than speed.

How Bubble Sort Works

1. Start at the beginning of the list.
2. Compare the first two elements. If the first element is greater than the second element, swap them.
3. Move to the next pair of elements (i.e., elements at index 2 and 3) and repeat the comparison and swapping if necessary.
4. Continue this process, moving one step at a time through the list, until you reach the end. This completes one pass.
5. Repeat steps 1 to 4 for a total of n-1 passes, where n is the number of elements in the list.
6. After n-1 passes, the largest element will have "bubbled up" to the end of the list.
7. Repeat the entire process, but this time exclude the last (already sorted) element.
8. Continue this process for n-2 passes, then n-3 passes, and so on, until the entire list is sorted.

Example of Bubble Sort

Let's walk through a simple example of bubble sort to understand how it works. Consider the following unsorted list:

[5, 1, 4, 2, 8]

1. In the first pass, we compare adjacent elements and swap if necessary. After the first pass, the largest element (8) is at the end of the list.
    o   [1, 4, 2, 5, 8]
2. In the second pass, we exclude the last element (8) since it's already sorted. We compare and swap elements as needed.
    o   [1, 2, 4, 5, 8]
3. After the third pass, the list is fully sorted.

Time Complexity

Bubble sort has a time complexity of $O(n^2)$, where n is the number of elements in the list. This means that as the size of the list increases, the time it takes to sort the list grows quadratically. Therefore, bubble sort is inefficient for large datasets and is generally not recommended for practical use when more efficient sorting algorithms like quicksort or merge sort are available.

When to Use Bubble Sort

Bubble sort is mainly used for educational purposes to illustrate the concept of sorting algorithms due to its simplicity. It can also be used for very small lists where efficiency is not a significant concern. In practice, for sorting large datasets or in performance-critical applications, more efficient sorting algorithms are preferred.

Selection Sort

Selection Sort is a simple comparison-based sorting algorithm that works by repeatedly selecting the minimum element from the unsorted portion of the list and moving it to the beginning of the sorted portion. It's one of the simplest sorting algorithms and is easy to understand and implement. However, it is not the most efficient sorting algorithm for large datasets and is primarily used for educational purposes or when simplicity is more important than speed.

How Selection Sort Works

1. Divide the list into two parts: the sorted portion and the unsorted portion. Initially, the sorted portion is empty, and the entire list is unsorted.

2. In each pass, find the minimum element in the unsorted portion of the list.
3. Swap the minimum element with the leftmost (first) element of the unsorted portion, effectively expanding the sorted portion.
4. Repeat steps 2 and 3 for each pass until the entire list is sorted.

Example of Selection Sort

Let's walk through an example of selection sort to understand how it works. Consider the following unsorted list:

[64, 25, 12, 22, 11]

1. In the first pass, the minimum element in the unsorted portion is 11. We swap it with the leftmost element (64).
   o   [11, 25, 12, 22, 64]
2. In the second pass, the minimum element in the remaining unsorted portion is 12. We swap it with the leftmost element (25).
   o   [11, 12, 25, 22, 64]
3. In the third pass, the minimum element in the remaining unsorted portion is 22. We swap it with the leftmost element (25).
   o   [11, 12, 22, 25, 64]
4. In the fourth pass, the minimum element in the remaining unsorted portion is 25. We swap it with the leftmost element (64).
   o   [11, 12, 22, 25, 64]
5. The list is now fully sorted.

Time Complexity

Selection sort has a time complexity of $O(n^2)$, where n is the number of elements in the list. This makes it inefficient for large datasets, as the time required to sort the list grows quadratically with the number of elements. Therefore, selection sort is generally not recommended for practical use when more efficient sorting algorithms like quicksort or merge sort are available.

When to Use Selection Sort

Selection sort is primarily used for educational purposes to introduce the concept of sorting algorithms and their basic principles. It can also be used for very small lists where efficiency is not a significant concern. In practice, for sorting large datasets or in performance-critical applications, more efficient sorting algorithms are preferred.

Insertion Sort

Insertion Sort is a simple and efficient comparison-based sorting algorithm that builds the final sorted array one element at a time. It works by repeatedly taking an unsorted element and inserting it into its correct position within the sorted portion of the array. Insertion sort is particularly efficient for small lists and lists that are nearly sorted. It is easy to understand and implement, making it a suitable choice for certain scenarios.

How Insertion Sort Works

Insertion sort divides the array into two parts: the sorted portion and the unsorted portion. Initially, the sorted portion contains only the first element, and the unsorted portion contains the remaining elements. The algorithm then iterates through the unsorted portion, taking one element at a time and inserting it into its correct position within the sorted portion.

Here are the steps of insertion sort:

1. Start with the second element (index 1) as the first element is considered sorted by default.
2. Compare the current element with the elements in the sorted portion from right to left.
3. Shift the elements in the sorted portion to the right until the correct position for the current element is found.
4. Insert the current element into its correct position in the sorted portion.
5. Repeat steps 2 to 4 for each remaining element in the unsorted portion.
6. Continue this process until the entire array is sorted.

Example of Insertion Sort

Let's walk through an example of insertion sort to understand how it works. Consider the following unsorted list:

[64, 25, 12, 22, 11]

1. We start with the second element (25) and compare it with the first element (64). Since 25 is smaller, we shift 64 one position to the right and insert 25.
   o [25, 64, 12, 22, 11]
2. We move to the next unsorted element (12) and compare it with the elements in the sorted portion. We shift 64 and 25 to the right and insert 12.
   o [12, 25, 64, 22, 11]
3. We continue this process for the remaining elements, shifting and inserting each element into its correct position.

- o [12, 22, 25, 64, 11]
- o [11, 12, 22, 25, 64]
4. The list is now fully sorted.

Time Complexity

Insertion sort has an average and worst-case time complexity of $O(n^2)$, where n is the number of elements in the list. While it is not the most efficient sorting algorithm for large datasets, its performance can be quite good for small lists and nearly sorted lists. It has a linear time complexity of $O(n)$ for already sorted lists, making it an excellent choice in such cases.

When to Use Insertion Sort

Insertion sort is a suitable choice when:

- You are working with small lists or datasets.
- The list is nearly sorted or partially sorted.
- Simplicity and ease of implementation are more important than sorting speed.

In practice, insertion sort is often used as part of more complex algorithms or combined with other sorting techniques.

Merge Sort

Merge Sort is an efficient and stable comparison-based sorting algorithm that follows the divide-and-conquer paradigm. It works by recursively dividing the unsorted list into smaller sublists, sorting each sublist, and then merging the sorted sublists to produce a final sorted array. Merge Sort is known for its consistent performance and is often used as the basis for other efficient sorting algorithms.

How Merge Sort Works

Merge Sort operates through a series of recursive steps:

1. **Divide:** The unsorted list is divided into two halves, typically by finding the midpoint of the list. This process continues until each sublist contains only one element, which is inherently sorted.
2. **Conquer:** The sorted sublists are then merged together in pairs. In each pair, the elements are compared, and a new sorted sublist is created. This process continues until there is only one sorted sublist remaining, which is the final sorted array.

3. **Merge**: The merging process involves comparing elements from the two sublists and placing them in the correct order in a new temporary list. This temporary list eventually replaces the original unsorted list, resulting in a sorted array.

Here's a high-level overview of the merge sort process:

1. **Divide** the unsorted list into two halves.
2. **Conquer** by recursively sorting the two halves.
3. **Merge** the sorted halves into a single sorted list.

Example of Merge Sort

Let's walk through an example of merge sort to understand how it works. Consider the following unsorted list:

[38, 27, 43, 3, 9, 82, 10]

1. Divide the list into two halves:
    o   Left sublist: [38, 27, 43, 3]
    o   Right sublist: [9, 82, 10]
2. Recursively sort each sublist:
    o   Left sublist:
        ▪   Divide: [38, 27]
        ▪   Recursively sort: [27, 38]
    o   Right sublist:
        ▪   Divide: [9, 82, 10]
        ▪   Recursively sort: [9, 10, 82]
3. Merge the sorted sublists:
    o   Left sublist: [27, 38]
    o   Right sublist: [9, 10, 82]

    Merging these two sorted sublists results in the final sorted list:

    o   [9, 10, 27, 38, 43, 82]

The list is now fully sorted.

Time Complexity

Merge Sort is known for its efficient time complexity, making it suitable for large datasets. It has a consistent time complexity of $O(n \log n)$, where n is the number of elements in the list. This performance is achieved because Merge Sort divides the list into halves, resulting in a balanced tree of recursive calls. It is a stable sorting algorithm, meaning it maintains the relative order of equal elements.

When to Use Merge Sort

Merge Sort is a good choice when:

- You require a stable sorting algorithm that maintains the relative order of equal elements.
- You need a sorting algorithm with a consistent and efficient time complexity, making it suitable for large datasets.
- You have enough memory available to handle the temporary storage required during the merge step.

Merge Sort is often used in practice, especially in scenarios where stability and predictable performance are crucial, such as sorting large databases or implementing external sorting for very large datasets.

Quick Sort

Quick Sort is a highly efficient and widely used comparison-based sorting algorithm that follows the divide-and-conquer paradigm. It works by selecting a "pivot" element from the unsorted list and partitioning the other elements into two sublists: elements less than the pivot and elements greater than the pivot. These sublists are then recursively sorted. Quick Sort is known for its average-case time complexity of O(n log n), making it one of the fastest sorting algorithms for most practical scenarios.

How Quick Sort Works

Quick Sort operates through a series of recursive steps:

1. **Pivot Selection**: Choose a pivot element from the unsorted list. The choice of pivot can affect the algorithm's performance.
2. **Partitioning**: Rearrange the elements in the list so that elements less than the pivot are on its left, and elements greater than the pivot are on its right. The pivot is now in its final sorted position.
3. **Recursion**: Recursively apply Quick Sort to the sublists created on the left and right sides of the pivot until the entire list is sorted.

Here's a high-level overview of the Quick Sort process:

1. **Select a pivot element** from the unsorted list.
2. **Partition the list** into two sublists: elements less than the pivot and elements greater than the pivot.
3. **Recursively apply Quick Sort** to the sublists on the left and right of the pivot.
4. Combine the sorted sublists and the pivot to produce the final sorted list.

Example of Quick Sort

Let's walk through an example of Quick Sort to understand how it works. Consider the following unsorted list:

[38, 27, 43, 3, 9, 82, 10]

1. Select a pivot element. In this case, we'll choose the last element, which is 10.
2. Partition the list into two sublists:
   - Left sublist (elements less than the pivot): [3, 9]
   - Right sublist (elements greater than the pivot): [38, 27, 43, 82]
3. Recursively apply Quick Sort to the sublists:
   - Left sublist: [3, 9] (already sorted)
   - Right sublist: [27, 38, 43, 82]
4. Combine the sorted sublists and the pivot to produce the final sorted list:
   - [3, 9, 10, 27, 38, 43, 82]

The list is now fully sorted.

Time Complexity

Quick Sort has an average-case time complexity of $O(n \log n)$, which makes it one of the fastest sorting algorithms for most practical scenarios. However, its worst-case time complexity is $O(n^2)$, which occurs when the pivot selection leads to consistently unbalanced partitions. To mitigate this, various pivot selection strategies are used in practice.

When to Use Quick Sort

Quick Sort is a good choice when:

- You need a highly efficient sorting algorithm with an average-case time complexity of $O(n \log n)$.
- You have enough memory to handle the recursive calls (it has a space complexity of $O(\log n)$).
- You can choose a good pivot selection strategy to minimize the risk of worst-case behavior.

Quick Sort is widely used in practice and is often the default choice for sorting algorithms in many programming languages and libraries due to its excellent average-case performance.

Comparison of Sorting Algorithms

Choosing the right sorting algorithm for a specific task depends on various factors, including the size of the dataset, the distribution of data, memory constraints, and the desired time complexity.

1. Bubble Sort, Selection Sort, and Insertion Sort:

- **Strengths:**
  - o Simple to understand and implement.
  - o Efficient for small datasets or nearly sorted lists.
- **Weaknesses:**
  - o Inefficient for large datasets ($O(n^2)$ time complexity).
  - o Not suitable for highly unsorted lists.
- **Use Cases:**
  - o Educational purposes.
  - o Small lists or mostly sorted lists where simplicity is more important than speed.

2. Merge Sort:

- **Strengths:**
  - o Efficient and stable with a consistent $O(n \log n)$ time complexity.
  - o Suitable for large datasets.
  - o Suitable for external sorting.
- **Weaknesses:**
  - o Requires additional memory for temporary storage.
- **Use Cases:**
  - o General-purpose sorting for large datasets.
  - o Stable sorting requirements.

3. Quick Sort:

- **Strengths:**
  - o Highly efficient with an average-case $O(n \log n)$ time complexity.
  - o In-place sorting (minimal additional memory).
  - o Widely used in practice.
- **Weaknesses:**

- o   Worst-case time complexity of O(n^2) when not well-pivoted.
- **Use Cases:**
  - o   General-purpose sorting for large datasets.
  - o   Default choice in many programming languages and libraries.

4. Heap Sort:

- **Strengths:**
  - o   Efficient with a consistent O(n log n) time complexity.
  - o   In-place sorting.
- **Weaknesses:**
  - o   Slightly slower in practice than Quick Sort and Merge Sort.
- **Use Cases:**
  - o   Sorting with strict memory constraints.
  - o   Heaps are already available (e.g., priority queue operations).

5. Radix Sort, Counting Sort, and Bucket Sort:

- **Strengths:**
  - o   Efficient for specific scenarios with known data characteristics.
  - o   Linear time complexity (O(n)) for certain cases.
- **Weaknesses:**
  - o   Limited to specific data types and distributions.
  - o   Not suitable for general-purpose sorting.
- **Use Cases:**
  - o   Integer sorting with a known range.
  - o   External sorting when keys are uniformly distributed.

6. Comparison Summary:

- For small datasets or nearly sorted lists, consider Bubble Sort, Selection Sort, or Insertion Sort.
- For general-purpose sorting with good average-case performance, Quick Sort and Merge Sort are solid choices.
- Use Merge Sort when stability is important or when sorting large datasets.
- Quick Sort is a popular general-purpose choice for its speed and practicality.
- Heap Sort is efficient and in-place but may be slightly slower than Quick Sort and Merge Sort.
- Radix Sort, Counting Sort, and Bucket Sort are specialized algorithms for specific scenarios with known data characteristics.

SEARCHING ALGORITHMS

Linear Search

Linear Search, also known as sequential search, is one of the simplest and most intuitive searching algorithms. It works by examining each element in a dataset one by one until the desired element is found or the entire dataset has been searched. While linear search is straightforward, it may not be the most efficient choice for large datasets, especially when compared to more advanced searching algorithms like binary search or hash-based methods.

How Linear Search Works

Linear search follows a straightforward procedure:

1. **Start at the beginning of the dataset** (usually the first element).
2. **Compare the current element with the target element** you are searching for.
3. If the current element matches the target, **return its index** (or position) in the dataset.
4. If the current element does not match the target, **move to the next element** in the dataset and repeat steps 2 and 3.
5. Continue this process until the target element is found or until the end of the dataset is reached, indicating that the element is not present.

Example of Linear Search

Let's walk through an example of linear search to understand how it works. Consider the following dataset:

[12, 34, 54, 2, 7, 19, 23, 45]

Suppose we want to search for the element 19.

1. Start at the beginning of the dataset, which is 12. Since 12 is not the target element (19), we move to the next element (34).
2. We continue comparing each element with the target:
   - o 54 (not the target)
   - o 2 (not the target)
   - o 7 (not the target)
   - o 19 (found the target)
3. We return the index of the found element, which is 5.

Linear search has successfully located the target element 19 in the dataset.

Time Complexity

Linear search has a time complexity of O(n), where n is the number of elements in the dataset. This means that the time it takes to search for an element increases linearly with the size of the dataset. For small datasets or when searching for elements near the beginning of the list, linear search can be efficient. However, for large datasets, it may not be the most time-effective choice.

When to Use Linear Search

Linear search is suitable when:

- The dataset is small.
- You do not know whether the data is sorted or not.
- You need to find the first occurrence of an element in the dataset.

In practice, linear search is often used when searching for items in unsorted lists or arrays, as it is straightforward to implement and requires minimal additional memory.

Binary Search

Binary Search is a highly efficient searching algorithm that works by repeatedly dividing a sorted dataset in half and comparing the middle element to the target element. By systematically eliminating half of the dataset with each comparison, binary search can locate a target element in logarithmic time, making it one of the fastest searching algorithms for sorted data.

How Binary Search Works

Binary search follows a systematic process:

1. **Start with a sorted dataset**: Binary search requires the dataset to be sorted in ascending or descending order.
2. **Initialize pointers**: Set two pointers, one at the beginning of the dataset (left pointer) and another at the end (right pointer).
3. **Find the middle element**: Calculate the middle index of the dataset by averaging the left and right pointers (e.g., (left + right) / 2).
4. **Compare the middle element with the target element**:
    o   If the middle element matches the target, **the search is successful**, and you return its index (or position).
    o   If the middle element is greater than the target, **move the right pointer to the middle index - 1**, effectively eliminating the right half of the dataset.
    o   If the middle element is less than the target, **move the left pointer to the middle index + 1**, effectively eliminating the left half of the dataset.
5. **Repeat steps 3 and 4** until the target element is found or the left pointer surpasses the right pointer, indicating that the element is not present in the dataset.

Example of Binary Search

Let's walk through an example of binary search to understand how it works. Consider the following sorted dataset:

csharp
[2, 7, 12, 19, 23, 34, 45, 54]

Suppose we want to search for the element 19.

1. Initialize the left pointer at the beginning of the dataset (index 0) and the right pointer at the end (index 7).
2. Calculate the middle index: (0 + 7) / 2 = 3. The middle element is 19.
3. Compare 19 with the target 19. Since they match, the search is successful, and we return the index 3.

Binary search has successfully located the target element 19 in the dataset.

Time Complexity

Binary search has a time complexity of O(log n), where n is the number of elements in the sorted dataset. This makes it an extremely efficient searching algorithm, particularly for large datasets. The logarithmic time complexity means that the time required to search for an element increases much slower than the size of the dataset.

When to Use Binary Search

Binary search is suitable when:

- The dataset is sorted.
- You have a large dataset, and you need to locate an element efficiently.
- You can afford to sort the dataset initially, as the sorting process takes O(n log n) time for typical sorting algorithms like Quick Sort or Merge Sort.

In practice, binary search is widely used in various applications, including searching in databases, finding items in sorted lists, and determining positions in ordered data structures like arrays.

Hash-Based Search

Hash-Based Search is a searching approach that utilizes hash functions and data structures to efficiently locate and retrieve information from large datasets. It is particularly effective when the data is organized using hash tables or similar structures, enabling near-instantaneous access to stored values. Hash-based search is commonly used in databases, data retrieval systems, and various applications where quick data lookup is essential.

How Hash-Based Search Works

Hash-based search relies on the concept of hashing, which involves the use of a hash function to map data values to specific locations or addresses in a data structure, such as a hash table. Here's an overview of how hash-based search operates:

1. **Hash Function**: A hash function takes an input value (e.g., a key or identifier) and computes a hash code or hash value based on that input. The hash function should ideally produce a unique hash value for each unique input.
2. **Hash Table**: The data is organized in a data structure called a hash table. A hash table is an array-like structure where each element corresponds to a specific location, known as a bucket or slot.

3. **Hashing**: When you want to store or retrieve data, you apply the hash function to the data's key to determine its hash code. This hash code is then used to identify the appropriate bucket in the hash table.
4. **Storage and Retrieval**:
    o **Storage**: To store data, you calculate the hash code for the key, which indicates the target bucket. You place the data in that bucket.
    o **Retrieval**: When you want to retrieve data, you calculate the hash code for the key again. This hash code guides you directly to the correct bucket, where you can access the stored data without having to search through the entire dataset.
5. **Handling Collisions**: Hash functions may occasionally produce the same hash code for different keys, resulting in collisions. Hash tables typically have mechanisms to resolve collisions, such as chaining (using linked lists in each bucket) or open addressing (probing neighboring buckets).

Example of Hash-Based Search

Let's consider a simple example where you want to create a phonebook application that allows you to quickly look up phone numbers using people's names.

1. **Hash Function**: You design a hash function that takes a person's name as input and computes a unique hash code based on the name's characters. This hash code will map each name to a specific location in the hash table.
2. **Hash Table**: You set up a hash table with a predefined number of buckets. Each bucket will store a list of name-phone number pairs.
3. **Storage**: When someone's name and phone number are added to the phonebook, you apply the hash function to the name, which determines the appropriate bucket. You store the name and phone number in that bucket.
4. **Retrieval**: To find a phone number, you provide a name, apply the same hash function to compute the hash code, and use it to identify the bucket. Within that bucket, you search for the desired name and retrieve the associated phone number.

Advantages and Considerations

Hash-based search offers several advantages:

- **Fast Retrieval**: Hash-based search provides nearly instantaneous access to stored data, making it highly efficient for lookup operations.
- **Scalability**: It can handle large datasets efficiently as long as the hash function and data structure are designed appropriately.
- **Deterministic**: Given the same input key, the hash function will consistently produce the same hash code, ensuring predictable access.

However, there are some considerations:

- **Hash Function Design**: The quality of the hash function greatly influences the performance and avoidance of collisions.
- **Collisions**: Collisions can occur, requiring mechanisms like chaining or open addressing to handle them.
- **Memory Usage**: Hash tables can consume more memory than other data structures.

Interpolation Search

Interpolation Search is a searching algorithm that is particularly effective when searching for a specific target element in a dataset with uniformly distributed values. It is an improvement over binary search, especially when the dataset contains sorted, continuous, and evenly spaced values. Interpolation search takes advantage of this uniform distribution to estimate the likely position of the target element, reducing the number of comparisons required for successful retrieval.

How Interpolation Search Works

Interpolation search follows a systematic approach based on the estimation of the target element's position:

1. **Initialization**: Start with a sorted dataset and define the left and right bounds. These bounds initially encompass the entire dataset.
2. **Estimate the Position**: Calculate an estimated position for the target element based on its value relative to the minimum and maximum values in the dataset. This estimation is performed using a formula:

position = left + ((target - dataset[left]) * (right - left)) / (dataset[right] - dataset[left])

2. Here, target is the value you are searching for, left and right are the current bounds, and dataset[left] and dataset[right] are the minimum and maximum values in the dataset, respectively.
3. **Comparison**: Compare the estimated position with the actual value at that position in the dataset:
    - If the estimated value matches the target, the search is successful.
    - If the estimated value is less than the target, update the left bound to be one position to the right of the estimated position and repeat the process.
    - If the estimated value is greater than the target, update the right bound to be one position to the left of the estimated position and repeat the process.

4. **Repeat**: Continue estimating and comparing until the target element is found or until the left bound surpasses the right bound, indicating that the element is not present in the dataset.

Example of Interpolation Search

Let's walk through an example of interpolation search to understand how it works. Consider a sorted dataset of temperatures in Celsius:

[0, 10, 20, 30, 40, 50, 60, 70, 80, 90, 100]

Suppose we want to search for the temperature 70°C.

1. Initialization: Set the left bound to 0 and the right bound to 100.
2. Estimate the Position:

position = 0 + ((70 - 0) * (100 - 0)) / (100 - 0) = 70

2. The estimated position is 70.
3. Comparison: Compare the value at position 70 in the dataset with the target 70°C. They match, indicating a successful search.

Interpolation search has successfully located the target temperature 70°C in the dataset.

Time Complexity

The time complexity of interpolation search depends on the distribution of values in the dataset. In the best-case scenario, when the values are uniformly distributed, the time complexity approaches O(log log n). However, in the worst-case scenario (non-uniform distribution), it can be as bad as O(n), making it less efficient than binary search for datasets with irregular distributions.

When to Use Interpolation Search

Interpolation search is suitable when:

- The dataset is sorted.
- The values are uniformly distributed.
- You want to optimize searching for values that are more likely to be closer to certain positions in the dataset.

It's essential to consider the distribution of data when choosing between interpolation search and other searching algorithms like binary search or hash-based methods.

ADVANCED TOPICS

Dynamic Programming

Dynamic Programming is a powerful technique used in computer science and mathematics to solve complex problems by breaking them down into simpler overlapping subproblems. It involves solving each subproblem only once and storing the results to avoid redundant work, leading to significant time and space savings. Dynamic programming is particularly valuable when dealing with optimization problems and problems that exhibit optimal substructure and overlapping subproblems.

Key Concepts of Dynamic Programming

Dynamic programming relies on several key concepts:

1. **Optimal Substructure**: A problem exhibits optimal substructure when the optimal solution to the overall problem can be constructed from optimal solutions to its smaller subproblems. This property allows us to solve the problem incrementally.
2. **Overlapping Subproblems**: In many cases, the same subproblem is solved multiple times within the process of solving the larger problem. Dynamic programming addresses this issue by solving each subproblem only once and storing the results in a data structure like a table or an array.
3. **Memoization**: Memoization is the process of storing the results of expensive function calls and returning the cached result when the same inputs occur again. It is often used in top-down dynamic programming approaches.

4. **Tabulation**: Tabulation is the process of building a table (usually a two-dimensional array) from the bottom up, solving each subproblem iteratively. It is often used in bottom-up dynamic programming approaches.

Dynamic Programming Techniques

Dynamic programming encompasses several techniques, including:

1. **Top-Down (Memoization) Approach**: In this approach, you start with the original problem and recursively break it down into subproblems. You use memoization to store the results of subproblems so that they are computed only once. This approach is often implemented using recursion with a cache or a data structure like a dictionary.
2. **Bottom-Up (Tabulation) Approach**: In the bottom-up approach, you start by solving the smallest subproblems and build your way up to the original problem. You use an iterative loop to fill a table with results, avoiding the need for recursion. This approach is typically more efficient in terms of both time and space.

Practical Applications

Dynamic programming finds application in various domains, including:

- **Combinatorial Optimization**: Problems like the traveling salesman problem, the knapsack problem, and the longest common subsequence problem can be solved efficiently using dynamic programming.
- **Algorithm Optimization**: Dynamic programming can be used to optimize algorithms by eliminating redundant calculations. For example, the Fibonacci sequence can be computed much faster using dynamic programming.
- **Natural Language Processing**: Dynamic programming is used in natural language processing for tasks like machine translation, speech recognition, and text summarization.
- **Game Theory**: In game theory, dynamic programming is used to analyze and optimize strategies in games and decision-making processes.
- **Bioinformatics**: Dynamic programming plays a vital role in sequence alignment, phylogenetics, and other biological data analysis tasks.

Greedy Algorithms

Greedy Algorithms are a class of algorithms that make locally optimal choices at each step with the hope of finding a globally optimal solution. In other words, they prioritize the best immediate option without considering the consequences of that choice on future steps. Greedy algorithms are particularly useful for solving optimization problems where the goal is to find the best solution from a set of possible choices.

Key Characteristics of Greedy Algorithms

Greedy algorithms possess several key characteristics:

1. **Greedy Choice Property**: At each step of the algorithm, a greedy choice is made by selecting the best option based on some criteria. This choice is made without considering how it will affect future steps.
2. **Optimal Substructure**: Greedy algorithms rely on the problem exhibiting optimal substructure, meaning that the solution to the overall problem can be constructed from the solutions to its smaller subproblems.
3. **No Backtracking**: Once a decision is made, it is never reconsidered. Greedy algorithms do not backtrack or change their mind about previous choices.

Example Applications

Greedy algorithms are widely used in various applications, including:

1. **Minimum Spanning Tree**: In graph theory, algorithms like Kruskal's and Prim's are greedy algorithms used to find the minimum spanning tree of a graph, connecting all nodes with the minimum total edge weight.
2. **Dijkstra's Algorithm**: Dijkstra's algorithm, a popular greedy algorithm, finds the shortest path between nodes in a weighted graph. It iteratively selects the node with the smallest tentative distance from the source node.
3. **Huffman Coding**: Huffman coding is a lossless data compression algorithm that uses a greedy approach to construct variable-length codes for characters in a text. Frequent characters are assigned shorter codes.
4. **Fractional Knapsack Problem**: In the fractional knapsack problem, the goal is to maximize the value of items placed in a knapsack with a limited weight capacity. Greedy algorithms can be used to select items based on their value-to-weight ratio.
5. **Interval Scheduling**: Greedy algorithms are used to solve interval scheduling problems, where the goal is to select the maximum number of non-overlapping intervals from a given set.

Advantages and Limitations

Greedy algorithms have several advantages:

- They are often simple to understand and implement.
- They can be efficient in terms of time complexity.

- They work well for certain types of problems with optimal substructure.

However, they also have limitations:

- Greedy algorithms may not always guarantee the globally optimal solution. They can lead to suboptimal solutions in some cases.
- It's essential to choose the right greedy criteria for a specific problem; otherwise, the algorithm may fail to produce the desired results.
- Greedy algorithms do not work for problems that lack the greedy choice property, where the locally optimal choices do not lead to a globally optimal solution.

Divide and Conquer

Divide and Conquer is a powerful algorithmic paradigm used to solve complex problems by breaking them down into smaller, more manageable subproblems. The approach involves three fundamental steps: divide, conquer, and combine. Divide and Conquer algorithms are known for their efficiency and are widely used in various domains, including computer science, mathematics, and engineering.

Key Concepts of Divide and Conquer

Divide and Conquer algorithms rely on several key concepts:

1. **Divide**: The original problem is divided into smaller, independent subproblems that are similar in nature to the original problem but on a reduced scale. The goal is to break down the problem into smaller, more manageable pieces.
2. **Conquer**: Each subproblem is solved independently. In some cases, subproblems may be small enough to be solved directly. In other cases, they are solved recursively, using the same algorithm.
3. **Combine**: Once the subproblems are solved, their solutions are combined to form the solution to the original problem. This step is often called the "merge" or "combine" phase.

Examples of Divide and Conquer Algorithms

Divide and Conquer algorithms find application in various fields and are used to solve a wide range of problems, including:

1. **Merge Sort**: A classic sorting algorithm that divides an unsorted array into two halves, recursively sorts each half, and then merges the sorted halves back together.

2. **Quick Sort**: Another sorting algorithm that selects a "pivot" element from the array and divides the array into two subarrays: elements less than the pivot and elements greater than the pivot. It recursively sorts the subarrays.

3. **Binary Search**: A search algorithm that divides a sorted array into two halves and compares the target element with the middle element. Depending on the comparison, it continues the search in the left or right half, effectively halving the search space at each step.

4. **Closest Pair of Points**: Given a set of points in a plane, this algorithm finds the pair of points with the smallest distance between them. It divides the points into two halves, recursively finds the closest pairs in each half, and then considers pairs that span the dividing line.

5. **Fast Fourier Transform (FFT)**: An efficient algorithm for multiplying two polynomials or performing discrete Fourier transforms. It recursively divides the problem into smaller subproblems.

Advantages and Limitations

Divide and Conquer algorithms offer several advantages:

- They are often highly efficient and can reduce the time complexity of a problem significantly.
- They are well-suited for parallel processing, as subproblems can be solved independently.
- They are a versatile approach and can be applied to various problems.

However, they also have limitations:

- Not all problems exhibit a natural division into subproblems with similar characteristics.
- The overhead of recursively dividing and combining subproblems can be significant for small problem instances.
- Careful analysis is required to determine whether a problem can be effectively solved using the Divide and Conquer approach.

NP-Completeness and Algorithms

NP-completeness is a fundamental concept in computer science and computational theory that classifies certain problems based on their computational complexity. Problems classified as NP-complete have a unique set of properties that make them both challenging and intriguing. Understanding NP-completeness is crucial for assessing the difficulty of solving computational problems and has far-reaching implications for algorithm design and optimization.

What is NP-Completeness?

NP stands for "nondeterministic polynomial time," which refers to a class of problems that can be verified in polynomial time. In other words, given a potential solution, you can quickly determine if it's correct.

A problem is **NP-complete** if it has two critical properties:

1. **Nondeterministic Polynomial Time Verification**: Given a potential solution, you can verify its correctness in polynomial time.
2. **Hardness**: If you can find a polynomial-time algorithm to solve one NP-complete problem, you can use it to solve all NP-complete problems in polynomial time. This means that NP-complete problems are, in a sense, the most challenging problems within NP.

Implications for Algorithms

The existence of NP-complete problems has profound implications for algorithm design and optimization:

1. **No Known Polynomial-Time Solutions**: While we can quickly verify a potential solution for an NP-complete problem, we have not yet discovered polynomial-time algorithms to solve them. Many famous problems, such as the Traveling Salesman Problem (TSP) and the Knapsack Problem, are NP-complete.
2. **Reducibility**: One of the key ideas in dealing with NP-completeness is **reducibility**. If you can show that a problem A can be reduced to another problem B (i.e., solving A efficiently can help you solve B efficiently), and B is NP-complete, then A is also NP-complete. This is the basis for proving that many problems are NP-complete.
3. **Implication for P vs. NP**: The most famous question in computer science is whether P (problems solvable in polynomial time) is equal to NP (problems verifiable in polynomial time). If P ≠ NP, it means that there are problems in NP for which no polynomial-time algorithms exist, including all NP-complete problems. This question remains unsolved and is one of the seven "Millennium Prize Problems" with a million-dollar reward for its solution.

Dealing with NP-Completeness

When faced with NP-complete problems, you have several options:

1. **Approximation Algorithms**: Since finding an exact solution efficiently might be impossible, you can design **approximation algorithms** that provide solutions that are close to optimal. These algorithms trade off accuracy for efficiency.
2. **Heuristics**: Heuristic algorithms provide a good solution quickly but do not guarantee optimality. They are often used for solving real-world instances of NP-complete problems.
3. **Special Cases**: Some NP-complete problems have efficient solutions when specific constraints or conditions are met. Identifying these conditions can be valuable.
4. **Parallel Computing**: Distributed and parallel computing can be employed to tackle NP-complete problems by dividing them into smaller tasks and solving them concurrently.

PERFORMANCE ANALYSIS

Time Complexity

Time complexity is a fundamental concept in computer science and algorithm analysis. It quantifies the amount of time an algorithm or program takes to execute in relation to the size of its input. Understanding time complexity is crucial for evaluating and comparing the efficiency of different algorithms, making informed algorithmic choices, and predicting how an algorithm will perform as the input size increases.

Why Time Complexity Matters

Efficiency is a critical consideration in software development and algorithm design for several reasons:

1. **Resource Usage**: In applications like web services, mobile apps, and embedded systems, resource usage, especially time, directly affects user experience. Faster algorithms lead to more responsive software.
2. **Scalability**: As data and input sizes grow, algorithms must remain efficient. Inefficient algorithms can quickly become impractical or even unusable with larger inputs.
3. **Cost**: In cloud computing and distributed systems, time translates to cost. More efficient algorithms can reduce the computational resources required and save money.
4. **Sustainability**: In energy-efficient computing, minimizing the time a processor is active can reduce power consumption, making algorithms more sustainable.

Big O Notation

Time complexity is often expressed using **Big O notation**, which provides an upper bound on the growth rate of an algorithm's runtime in relation to the input size. Common Big O notations include:

- **O(1)**: Constant time. The algorithm's runtime is independent of the input size.
- **O(log n)**: Logarithmic time. The algorithm's runtime grows slowly as the input size increases.
- **O(n)**: Linear time. The runtime is directly proportional to the input size.
- **O(n log n)**: Log-linear time. Common for many efficient sorting algorithms.
- **O(n^2)**: Quadratic time. The runtime grows with the square of the input size.
- **O(2^n)**: Exponential time. The runtime grows exponentially with the input size.

Analyzing Time Complexity

To determine the time complexity of an algorithm, follow these steps:

1. **Identify the Input Size**: Determine what constitutes the input size for your algorithm. For sorting algorithms, it's typically the number of elements to be sorted. For search algorithms, it's the size of the dataset being searched.
2. **Count Basic Operations**: Break down your algorithm into its fundamental operations and count how many times each operation is performed as a function of the input size.
3. **Express the Growth Rate**: Use Big O notation to express the upper bound of the algorithm's runtime in terms of the input size.
4. **Simplify**: Simplify the expression to its most significant term. For example, if an algorithm has a time complexity of O(n^2 + n), you would simplify it to O(n^2) because the n^2 term dominates the growth rate.

Comparing Algorithms

Time complexity analysis allows you to compare algorithms and make informed choices. When faced with multiple algorithms that solve the same problem, you can select the one with the most favorable time complexity for your specific use case.

Space Complexity

Space complexity is a critical concept in computer science and algorithm analysis. It quantifies the amount of memory or space an algorithm or program requires to execute in relation to the size of its input. Understanding space complexity is crucial for evaluating and comparing the memory efficiency of different algorithms, making informed algorithmic choices, and optimizing memory usage in software development.

The Significance of Space Complexity

Efficient memory usage is vital in modern computing for several reasons:

1. **Resource Constraints**: In embedded systems, mobile devices, and IoT devices, memory is often limited. Efficient algorithms and programs are essential to make the most of these constrained resources.
2. **Performance**: Efficient memory usage can improve program performance. Algorithms that use less memory may execute faster due to reduced data movement and cache usage.
3. **Scalability**: As datasets and input sizes grow, algorithms must manage memory efficiently. Programs with excessive memory consumption can fail or become impractical with large inputs.
4. **Cost**: In cloud computing and data centers, memory usage incurs costs. Reducing memory usage can lead to cost savings.

Space Complexity Analysis

To determine the space complexity of an algorithm, follow these steps:

1. **Identify Memory Usage**: Determine what data structures, variables, and auxiliary storage your algorithm uses. Include all memory allocations and data structures such as arrays, lists, and trees.
2. **Count Memory Consumption**: Analyze how the memory consumption grows as a function of the input size. Count the space required for each data structure and variable.
3. **Express the Growth Rate**: Use Big O notation to express the upper bound of the memory consumption in terms of the input size.
4. **Simplify**: Simplify the expression to its most significant term, just as you would with time complexity analysis.

Common Space Complexity Classes

Space complexity is often expressed using Big O notation, similar to time complexity. Common space complexity classes include:

- **O(1)**: Constant space. The algorithm uses a fixed, constant amount of memory, regardless of the input size.
- **O(log n)**: Logarithmic space. The space usage grows slowly as the input size increases.
- **O(n)**: Linear space. The memory usage is directly proportional to the input size.
- **O(n log n)**: Log-linear space. Common for many efficient sorting algorithms.
- **O(n^2)**: Quadratic space. The memory usage grows with the square of the input size.
- **O(2^n)**: Exponential space. The memory usage grows exponentially with the input size.

Optimizing Space Complexity

Optimizing space complexity often involves using data structures that minimize memory usage while still meeting the algorithm's requirements. Techniques such as in-place algorithms (where input data is modified rather than creating new data structures) and efficient memory management are essential for achieving low space complexity.

Balancing Time and Space

In algorithm design, there's often a trade-off between time complexity and space complexity. Algorithms that optimize for one may sacrifice efficiency in the other. Therefore, it's essential to strike a balance that meets the specific requirements of your application.

Big O Notation

Big O notation is a mathematical notation used in computer science and mathematics to describe the upper bound or worst-case behavior of an algorithm or function in terms of its input size. It provides a way to classify and compare the efficiency of algorithms and helps us understand how an algorithm's performance scales with larger inputs. Big O notation is a fundamental tool for algorithm analysis and plays a crucial role in algorithm design, optimization, and selection.

Why Big O Notation Matters

Big O notation is essential for several reasons:

1. **Algorithm Comparison**: It allows us to compare and contrast algorithms based on their efficiency and scalability. You can determine which algorithm is better suited for a specific problem by analyzing its Big O complexity.
2. **Performance Prediction**: Big O notation provides insight into how an algorithm will perform as the input size grows. This is invaluable for optimizing software and ensuring it can handle larger datasets.
3. **Resource Allocation**: In resource-constrained environments, such as embedded systems or cloud computing, understanding the resource requirements of algorithms is crucial for efficient resource allocation.
4. **Algorithmic Choices**: When designing software, selecting the right algorithm with an appropriate time complexity is critical for achieving the desired performance goals.

Key Notations in Big O

Big O notation uses several key notations to describe the growth rate of algorithms in terms of their input size:

- **O(1)**: Constant time. The algorithm's runtime or resource usage is constant and does not depend on the input size.
- **O(log n)**: Logarithmic time. The algorithm's performance grows very slowly as the input size increases.
- **O(n)**: Linear time. The algorithm's runtime or resource usage is directly proportional to the input size.
- **O(n log n)**: Log-linear time. Common for many efficient sorting algorithms. The growth rate is slightly faster than linear but still efficient.
- **O(n^2)**: Quadratic time. The algorithm's performance grows with the square of the input size. Often seen in nested loops.
- **O(2^n)**: Exponential time. The algorithm's performance grows exponentially with the input size. Typically considered inefficient for large inputs.

Analyzing Time Complexity with Big O

To determine the time complexity of an algorithm and express it using Big O notation, follow these steps:

1. **Identify Key Operations**: Identify the primary operations or steps within your algorithm that contribute most significantly to the runtime.
2. **Count Operations**: Count how many times these key operations are executed as a function of the input size.

3. **Express Complexity**: Use Big O notation to describe the upper bound of the number of operations or resource usage in terms of the input size.
4. **Simplify**: Simplify the expression to its most significant term to focus on the most critical factor affecting performance.

Practical Use of Big O Notation

Big O notation is widely used in the following practical scenarios:

- **Algorithm Selection**: Choose the most efficient algorithm for a specific problem based on its Big O complexity.
- **Performance Tuning**: Identify and optimize the most time-consuming parts of your code.
- **Scaling**: Evaluate how an algorithm will perform as data sizes grow to ensure that software can handle increased loads.
- **Resource Allocation**: Allocate resources efficiently in systems with limited resources.

Analyzing Algorithms

Analyzing algorithms is a fundamental skill for computer scientists and software developers. It involves evaluating the efficiency, correctness, and performance characteristics of algorithms to make informed design decisions. Proper algorithm analysis enables you to choose the right tool for the job, optimize code, and predict how software will perform under different conditions.

The Need for Algorithm Analysis

Why is analyzing algorithms important? Consider the following:

1. **Efficiency Matters**: In today's computing landscape, where we deal with vast amounts of data and complex computations, efficient algorithms are crucial. They save time, resources, and energy.
2. **Scalability**: Software often needs to handle ever-increasing datasets. Understanding how algorithms scale is essential for building systems that can grow with their demands.
3. **Resource Allocation**: In resource-constrained environments like embedded systems or cloud computing, optimizing algorithms is necessary for efficient resource utilization.
4. **Competitive Advantage**: In some cases, the efficiency of your algorithms can give you a competitive advantage, especially in industries like finance, where milliseconds matter.

Steps in Algorithm Analysis

Analyzing algorithms involves several steps:

1. **Identify the Goal**: Clearly define what you want to achieve with your algorithm. This could be solving a problem, sorting data, searching for information, or optimizing a process.
2. **Determine Inputs**: Understand the type and range of inputs your algorithm will work with. Consider best-case, average-case, and worst-case scenarios.
3. **Develop the Algorithm**: Create or select an algorithm that solves the problem. Ensure that it meets the required functionality and correctness criteria.
4. **Analyze Correctness**: First and foremost, verify that your algorithm produces the correct output for a range of test cases.
5. **Analyze Time Complexity**: Determine how the algorithm's runtime scales with input size. Use techniques such as Big O notation to express the upper bound of runtime.
6. **Analyze Space Complexity**: Assess the memory requirements of the algorithm. Use Big O notation to express the upper bound of memory usage.
7. **Benchmark and Profiling**: Conduct benchmarking and profiling to gather empirical data on your algorithm's performance in real-world scenarios.

Types of Algorithm Analysis

There are different types of algorithm analysis, including:

- **Asymptotic Analysis**: Focuses on the growth rate of algorithm performance as input size approaches infinity. It is expressed using Big O, Omega, and Theta notations.
- **Empirical Analysis**: Involves running experiments on the algorithm with real data to observe its actual performance under specific conditions.
- **Average-Case Analysis**: Determines the expected runtime of an algorithm when averaged over all possible inputs, considering their probabilities.
- **Worst-Case Analysis**: Assesses the algorithm's performance under the least favorable conditions, providing an upper bound on its runtime.
- **Best-Case Analysis**: Considers the algorithm's performance when it operates under the most favorable conditions, providing a lower bound on its runtime.

Optimization and Practicality

Algorithm analysis often leads to optimization efforts. Here are some optimization techniques:

- **Algorithmic Improvements**: Revisit and refine the algorithm to make it more efficient or reduce its space complexity.
- **Data Structures**: Select the right data structures to improve performance. For example, using a hash table for quick lookups.
- **Parallelism**: Explore opportunities for parallelism and concurrency in algorithms to leverage multiple processing units.
- **Memory Management**: Optimize memory usage through techniques like object pooling or reducing unnecessary allocations.

REAL-WORLD EXAMPLES OF USING DATA STRUCTURES AND ALGORITHMS IN C

1. **Databases and Indexing**:

    In database management systems, efficient data storage and retrieval are crucial. Data structures like B-trees and hash tables are commonly used to implement indexes, speeding up queries and data retrieval. For instance, in MySQL, B-trees are employed for indexing tables, ensuring fast searching and sorting of data.

2. **Operating Systems**:

    Operating systems like Linux and Windows rely heavily on data structures and algorithms. For example, the Linux kernel uses linked lists and trees to manage processes, files, and memory. Algorithms like the CFS (Completely Fair Scheduler) are used for task scheduling.

3. **Web Servers**:

    Web servers, such as Apache and Nginx, use various data structures and algorithms to efficiently handle client requests. Hash tables are used for fast URL lookup, and algorithms like round-robin are employed for load balancing.

4. **Network Routing**:

    In networking, routing algorithms are used to determine the best path for data packets to travel through a network. Dijkstra's algorithm and Bellman-

Ford are examples of algorithms used in routing protocols like OSPF and BGP.

5. **Graphics and Game Development**:

Video games and graphics applications require efficient data structures for rendering and processing. Quad trees and octrees are used for spatial partitioning, and algorithms like A* help find the shortest path for game characters.

6. **Search Engines**:

Search engines like Google employ complex data structures and algorithms to index and search through massive amounts of web content efficiently. Data structures like inverted indices and algorithms like PageRank are essential for ranking search results.

7. **Encryption and Security**:

Cryptographic algorithms rely on mathematical principles and data structures for secure communication. For example, the RSA algorithm uses prime numbers and modular arithmetic, while hash functions like SHA-256 use hash tables and bitwise operations.

8. **Machine Learning and AI**:

Machine learning algorithms often involve matrix operations, graph algorithms, and data structures like decision trees and neural networks. Libraries like TensorFlow and PyTorch use efficient C-based implementations to accelerate deep learning tasks.

9. **Image and Video Processing**:

Applications like Adobe Photoshop and video codecs utilize data structures like matrices and algorithms for image filtering, compression, and manipulation.

10. **Compiler Design**:

Compilers translate high-level programming languages into machine code. Lexical analysis, parsing, and optimization phases all involve complex algorithms and data structures like abstract syntax trees and symbol tables.

11. **File Systems**:

File systems like EXT4 and NTFS use data structures such as B-trees for organizing and managing file metadata and data blocks efficiently.

12. **Financial Software**:

Financial institutions rely on algorithms for risk assessment, portfolio optimization, and trading strategies. Data structures like arrays and linked lists are used for storing historical financial data.

13. **Embedded Systems**:

In resource-constrained environments, algorithms and data structures are essential for efficient memory and CPU usage. For instance, real-time operating systems like FreeRTOS use priority queues and task scheduling algorithms to manage system resources.

These examples demonstrate the pervasive role of data structures and algorithms in various domains of software development. They showcase the versatility and importance of these fundamental concepts in solving real-world problems and optimizing software performance.

COMMON C PROGRAMMING LIBRARIES

C is known for its simplicity and efficiency, but it lacks many of the high-level abstractions found in modern languages. To address this limitation and simplify development, C programmers often rely on libraries—collections of pre-written functions and modules that can be reused in various projects. Here are some common C programming libraries that can be incredibly valuable in your development endeavors:

1. Standard C Library (libc)

The Standard C Library, often referred to as libc, is the foundation of C programming. It provides essential functions and macros for tasks like input/output, memory allocation, string manipulation, and mathematical operations. Functions like printf(), scanf(), and malloc() are part of libc. This library is included with most C compilers and is available on nearly every C platform.

2. C Standard Template Library (STL)

The C++ Standard Template Library (STL) is a widely used library for C++ development, but it has been adapted for C as well. The C STL provides data structures like vectors, lists, and queues, along with algorithms for sorting, searching, and more. It's particularly useful when you want to use C's performance advantages but need some high-level data structures and algorithms.

3. OpenGL

If you're into graphics programming, OpenGL is a cross-platform graphics library that allows you to create 2D and 3D graphics. It's widely used in game development, simulations, and scientific visualization. While not exclusively a C library, it has C bindings, making it accessible to C programmers.

4. SQLite

SQLite is a self-contained, serverless, and zero-configuration SQL database engine. It's used extensively in embedded systems, mobile applications, and small-scale desktop applications. SQLite is written in C, but it has APIs for several programming languages, including C.

5. Pthreads (POSIX Threads)

Pthreads is a POSIX standard for multi-threading in C and C++. It allows you to create and manage threads in your programs. Multi-threading is essential for concurrent programming and can improve the performance of CPU-bound tasks. Pthreads provides functions for thread creation, synchronization, and communication.

6. CURL

CURL is a popular library for making network requests, supporting various protocols like HTTP, FTP, and more. It's often used for web scraping, downloading files, and interacting with web services. CURL provides a C API for making network requests from your C programs.

7. SDL (Simple DirectMedia Layer)

SDL is a cross-platform development library designed to provide low-level access to audio, keyboard, mouse, joystick, and graphics hardware. It's often used in game development, multimedia applications, and emulators. SDL has C bindings and can be used to create multimedia-rich C applications.

8. Math Library (libm)

The math library, libm, is an extension of the Standard C Library that provides mathematical functions for common operations like trigonometry, exponentiation, logarithms, and more. Functions like sin(), cos(), and exp() are part of libm.

9. OpenSSL

OpenSSL is a widely used open-source cryptographic library that provides secure socket layer (SSL) and transport layer security (TLS) protocols for securing network communications. While primarily written in C, it also has APIs for other languages, including C++ and Python.

10. GTK (GIMP Toolkit)

GTK is a popular multi-platform toolkit for creating graphical user interfaces (GUIs). It's the foundation for the GNOME desktop environment and is used for developing Linux desktop applications. GTK provides C bindings and is commonly used for creating Linux desktop applications.

These libraries extend the capabilities of the C programming language, allowing you to work on a wide range of projects, from low-level systems programming to high-level graphical applications. Depending on your project's requirements, you can leverage these libraries to simplify development and reduce the amount of code you need to write from scratch.

www.ingramcontent.com/pod-product-compliance
Lightning Source LLC
LaVergne TN
LVHW081346050326
832903LV00024B/1342